The Completion Agenda in Community Colleges

**THE ASSOCIATION OF COMMUNITY COLLEGE TRUSTEES
AND ROWMAN & LITTLEFIELD PUBLISHERS**

The Futures Series on Community Colleges

Sponsored by the Association of Community College Trustees and Rowman & Littlefield Publishers, *The Futures Series on Community Colleges* is designed to produce and deliver books that strike to the heart of issues that will shape the future of community colleges. *Futures* books examine emerging structures, systems and business models, and stretch prevailing assumptions about leadership and management by reaching beyond the limits of convention and tradition.

Topics addressed in the *series* are those that are vital to community colleges, but have yet to receive meaningful attention in literature, research, and analysis. *Futures* books are written by scholars and practitioners who deliver a unique perspective on a topic or issue—a president or higher education consultant bringing expert and practical understanding to a topic, a policy analyst breaking down a complex problem into component parts, an academic or think tank scholar conducting incisive research, or a researcher and a practitioner working together to examine an issue through different lenses.

Futures books are developed on the premise that disruptive innovation and industry transformation are, and will be, an ongoing challenge. Gradual improvement is, understandably, a natural preference of leaders. It will not be enough, however, to position our colleges for the future. The future will be about transformation and, to perform optimally, our colleges will need to become capable of large-scale change. As leaders come face-to-face with digital forces and rapidly changing social, economic and public policy conditions, they will have no choice but to get ahead of change or relinquish market position to competitors. *Futures* books are a vehicle through which leaders can learn about and prepare for what's ahead. Whether it's through analysis of what big data will mean in the next generation of colleges or which business models will become the new normal, *Futures* books are a resource for practitioners who realize that the ideas of out-of-the-box thinkers and the innovative practices of high performing organizations can be invaluable for answering big questions and solving complex problems.

Richard L. Alfred, Series Co-Editor
Emeritus Professor of Higher Education
University of Michigan

Debbie Sydow, Series Co-editor
President
Richard Bland College of the
College of William and Mary

Forthcoming Books in *The Futures Series on Community Colleges*

Developing Tomorrow's Leaders: Context, Challenges, and Capabilities
By Pamela Eddy, Debbie L. Sydow, Richard L. Alfred, and
Regina L. Garza Mitchell
   This book provides a template for leadership development in the community college sector. The theme of the book focuses on the need to move beyond hierarchical leadership to networked leadership that taps talent throughout the institution. The transformational change required in the two-year sector demands new approaches to leading, including tolerance for risk, use of data analytics, and a focus on relationships. New and alternative means for leadership development are presented.

The Urgency of Now: Equity and Excellence
By Marcus M. Kolb, Samuel D. Cargile, et al.
   The Urgency of Now asserts that in addition to being granted access to the community college, all 21st-century students need uncompromised support to succeed. Success means demonstrating relevant learning for transfer and employment, and timely completion of credentials. Looking to the future, the authors contend that community colleges, both by their past successes and future challenges, are at the epicenter for determining the essential ingredients of a new student-centered system that guarantees equity and excellence.

Unrelenting Change, Innovation, and Risk: Forging the Next Generation of Community Colleges
By Daniel J. Phelan
   In this book, thirty-five-year veteran Dan Phelan shares key insights from his personal and professional journey as a transformational, entrepreneurial community college leader. The book's wisdom and insights are amplified by observations gleaned from interviews and visits with dozens of leading practitioners. Drawing upon his sailing experiences, Phelan argues that leaders should stop playing it safe in the harbor because the real gains driving institutional and student success are found in uncharted waters. *Unrelenting Change, Innovation, and Risk* dares community college leaders to innovate and provides them with a toolkit for understanding changing conditions, assessing risk, and successfully navigating change.

Financing Community Colleges: Where We Are, Where We're Going
By Richard Romano and James Palmer

Grounded in an economic perspective, *Financing Community Colleges* helps college leaders make sense of the challenges they face in securing and managing the resources needed to carry out the community college mission. Finance has perpetually been an Achilles heel for leaders at all levels of management. With the premise that leaders are better at winning battles they know something about, this book equips leaders with an understanding of the fundamentals and the complexities of community college finance. It tackles current and emerging issues with insight that is analytic and prophetic—a must read for current and prospective leaders.

Institutional Analytics: Building a Culture of Evidence
By Karen Stout

Institutional Analytics paints a clear picture of the challenges involved in cultural change and building a team capable of using analytics to gain a competitive advantage for the future. Revealing that community colleges pretend to be more data driven than they actually are, Stout challenges leadership teams to set clear goals, define what success looks like, and ask the right questions to get there. By adopting new tools, abandoning legacy systems and relationships, and boldly adopting open source solutions, colleges can turn large quantities of data into business intelligence that drives transformation.

Previously Published Books in *The Series on Community Colleges*

Minding the Dream: The Process and Practice of the American Community College, Second Edition
By Gail O. Mellow and Cynthia M. Heelan
First in the World: Community Colleges and America's Future
By J. Noah Brown
Community College Student Success: From Boardrooms to Classrooms
By Banessa Smith Morest
Re-visioning Community Colleges
By Debbie Sydow and Richard Alfred
Community Colleges on the Horizon: Challenge, Choice, or Abundance
By Richard Alfred, Christopher Shults, Ozan Jaquette, and Shelley Strickland

The Completion Agenda in Community Colleges

What It Is, Why It Matters, and Where It's Going

Christopher Baldwin

Series Coeditors

Richard L. Alfred and Debbie L. Sydow

Rowman & Littlefield

Lanham • Boulder • New York • London

Published by Rowman & Littlefield
A wholly owned subsidiary of The Rowman & Littlefield Publishing Group, Inc.
4501 Forbes Boulevard, Suite 200, Lanham, Maryland 20706
www.rowman.com

Unit A, Whitacre Mews, 26-34 Stannary Street, London SE11 4AB

British Library Cataloguing in Publication Information Available

Library of Congress Cataloging-in-Publication Data

Names: Baldwin, Christopher, 1971– author.
Title: The completion agenda in community colleges : what it is, why it matters, and where it's going / Christopher Baldwin ; with Richard L. Alfred and Debbie L. Sydow.
Description: Lanham, Maryland : Rowman & Littlefield, 2017. | Series: The futures series on community colleges | Includes bibliographical references and index. |
Identifiers: LCCN 2017005864 (print) | LCCN 2017015959 (ebook) | ISBN 9781475809497 (Electronic) | ISBN 9781475809480 (cloth : alk. paper) | ISBN 9781475820683 (pbk. : alk. paper)
Subjects: LCSH: Community colleges—United States—Administration. | Community college graduates—United States. | Educational surveys—United States.
Classification: LCC LB2341 (ebook) | LCC LB2341 .B2725 2017 (print) | DDC 378.1/5430973—dc23
LC record available at https://lccn.loc.gov/2017005864

♾™ The paper used in this publication meets the minimum requirements of American National Standard for Information Sciences—Permanence of Paper for Printed Library Materials, ANSI/NISO Z39.48-1992.

Printed in the United States of America

Contents

List of Tables

Foreword

I want to begin by thanking my colleague and longtime friend Dr. Christopher Baldwin for inviting me to write this foreword. We've been partners on this work over the past decade, and his work individually and with his colleagues at Jobs for the Future and the Michigan Student Success Center has significantly and measurably advanced the guided pathways and completion movements. We are both fortunate to be part of a collaboration of national assistance partners in the guided pathways movement that has spent the past six-plus years in the trenches working alongside colleges, states, and foundations alike to move the needle on student outcomes in increasingly scaled and fundamental ways. Having played a leadership role in the student completion efforts in community colleges for over a decade, Chris is uniquely qualified to reflect on this movement in a way that effectively weaves theory and practice.

This is an important and impactful book; those involved in shepherding the national completion and improvement agenda in the community college space are keenly aware of the delicate balance that Chris aptly describes about what we may gain via the completion agenda and also the potential unintended consequences of a myopic focus on completion without a keen awareness of the impact on equity and access. Unfortunately, much of this nuance has only been shared in dialogues with large and small groups of practitioners and those who support them and it hasn't as often made it into written materials, such as this book. In addition, Chris has woven in a fascinating perspective on this work—that of the competing logics that guide and support how we think about the goals of our institutions and what these logics mean for scaling completion reform efforts.

Chris grounds the inquiry into these issues by clearly stating the goals—or at least what the goals should be—of the completion movement: that significantly more students achieve their primary goals of transfer to a four-year institution with junior standing in a major with no credit loss *or* direct entry into the workforce with credentials or degrees with marketplace value that ensure a living wage and a career path. He also points out that we sometimes lose sight of these goals as we get mired in the complexity of the cultural and practical change efforts that are required to significantly move the needle to achieve them.

At the heart of Chris's book is an exploration of the unintended potential consequences of the shift from an institutional logic based on access to one that tries to balance access based on success. As Chris points out, while this shift comes with a plethora of practice and policy changes needed to support the movement, those in the field must identify and combat unintended consequences that disadvantage the students who we are trying to effectively serve. The key point here is that this is a significant paradigm shift, and while the benefits of the new "logic" may very well result in the successful outcomes that we hope for our students, there is organizational change that is occurring that needs scaffolding and shepherding.

In addition to the logics frame Chris shares, he also introduces key structural tensions between the access and success logics in a number of important areas—college for all, comprehensiveness, resources, and instruction. These tensions are all interconnected; I've always viewed them as levers in a comprehensive system, except that it isn't always clear what happens when you move one lever higher or lower—the others may stay the same, move in parallel, or move in opposite directions. In my view, it requires vigilance both to the global outcomes you are endeavoring to improve as well as to the unintended consequences that in many ways are at the heart of Chris's book. We need to name the consequences we are most concerned about and take steps to ensure that they don't manifest in ways that would negatively affect students. In places where we cannot control for the unintended consequences, we have to strategize ways to mitigate the impact on students.

Chris has focused on two concerning unintended consequences: equity and quality. Citing national research and the concerns of presidents, Chris reminds us that our goals of community college completion of transfer with junior standing or direct entry into living wage jobs *need to be realized by all students*, not just the ones for whom the traditional model has been more successful. While we aren't happy with completion rates under the traditional model overall, some subpopulations have fared better than others—notably white students and students from the upper quartile of income level. As we work diligently to improve completion rates for all student groups, it is incumbent on us as professionals to pay close attention to the new "success logic" and ensure that the policies designed to achieve this success don't unintentionally shut out minority and low-income students.

Even further, Chris points out that it is the marketplace value of the credentials that ultimately matters—and we have to make sure that a "rush to completion" doesn't result in especially low-income and minority students receiving credentials that have lower or no marketplace value. This "false positive" completion is a significant concern, and it is important that Chris names it as a theme in this book. The good news from where I sit is that institutions such as Georgia State University and Valencia Community College that have markedly improved completion rates have also been laser focused on the issue of equity. These institutions have found the opposite—that the changes to culture, policy, and practice actually have a *bigger* effect on historically underrepresented groups. The impact on access and equity needs to be continually monitored throughout implementation of completion reforms and as new structures are brought to scale, and we have to make adjustments and improvements if the new models do not advantage all student populations.

Chris then explores the issue of quality and its relationship to the developments of the last decade on accountability and performance funding. I think there are two primary reasons to be skeptical of performance funding models (among many). One of these Chris mentions, which is that it's really challenging to set up a performance funding model that rewards the right behaviors in equitable ways across the range of institutions they cover even within a single state; no matter how you set it up, some colleges are advantaged and some are disadvantaged.

My other reason for skepticism is that, even if we didn't think of it this way, we have already been performance funded for years by incremental tuition and state funding. That is, when students are more successful in courses and persist and progress through programs of study toward completion/graduation/transfer, the college experiences incremental revenue from tuition and state funding (in all but a few states, where colleges don't keep their tuition revenue and state funding is not based on FTES). There are many additional questions associated with this mindset that need to be explored in other venues, but suffice it to say that I share Chris's conclusion that there is the potential for a number of perverse unintended consequences of performance funding models, perhaps without the flip side of the benefits that the models were purported to have—some of which haven't come to pass and some of which were already in existence.

Through his exploration of accountability and performance funding, Chris also explores the issue of academic quality. He mentions that it's a concern that the accountability and completion movement could result in a "watering down" of the curriculum or a lowering of standards. I have to say that while I agree that this is a potential concern, my work on the ground with over 325 colleges convinces me that while we tend to worry about this at a 35,000-foot level, the faculty as a whole are incredibly committed to ensuring that this is not an outcome of any improvement movement, including the guided pathways and completion movements. I do think that it's possible that one unintended consequence of the completion movement could be that a sole focus on completion narrowly defined might deemphasize a focus on teaching and learning and the associated professional development structures to support it, which would at the very least hinder efforts to *improve* quality as we move forward.

Finally, Chris explores two recent shifts in the field: the emergence of the guided pathways movement and the creation of student success centers in thirteen states. Both have the potential to move the field forward on the completion agenda, while also ensuring that we are mindful of how the policies and cultural changes associated with it could produce unintended consequences. Having participated in both of these shifts, I do share Chris's belief that the guided pathways movement can help focus college reform efforts on the end game he discusses and also help ensure that the potential unintended consequences don't come to pass. The Student Success Centers are clearly a galvanizing force in the states that have them; the remaining thirty-seven states can learn much from their approaches and try to formally or informally create or adapt such structures within their states.

I'd also be remiss not to share one of my favorite parts of this book: to make this book much more grounded in reality, Chris has infused key chapters with interviews and illustrative quotes from community college presidents from a Midwestern state that has been involved in the pathways movement and the completion agenda over the past ten years. While of course a small sample size, their words provide a poignant window into the issues their colleges face and how they view these issues. It is from both the similarities between these presidents' observations and the intriguing differences in their perception that we learn much about how leadership and college cultures interact in the trenches of the reform movement. Chris then weaves their insights on the completion agenda through the lenses of the competing logics and also the structural tensions noted above.

In sum, I think that this book is an incredibly important and thoughtful investigation of the intersection between the completion and guided pathways movements and the cultural and policy changes that are necessary to make this shift happen. He thoughtfully weaves together policy, practice, and theory and grounds it in the real perceptions of community college presidents. In doing so, he has helped us refocus on the mission of these movements as well as their promise, and it makes me more optimistic and excited that the path we will take to achieve these goals will have its intended results of positively changing the outcomes and lives of millions of students in this country in the not-too-distant future.

Rob Johnstone
President, National Center for Inquiry and Improvement
October 2016

Acknowledgments

As with any large undertaking, there are many people who have contributed to this book. I would like to start by thanking the countless practitioners and policymakers I have had the pleasure of working with over the past decade. Their dedication and commitment to the students they serve have been front and center as they have worked to reform community colleges and improve outcomes. More specifically, I would like to thank the college presidents I interviewed. Without them this book would not have been possible. I appreciate them taking time from their busy schedules to talk with me and for sharing their honest opinions about the challenges and opportunities they face. The role of a college president can be difficult and unappreciated, and I have been inspired by the professionalism and passion these individuals bring to their work.

I would also like to express my appreciation to a group of individuals who I consider to be sibling-colleagues—Michael Collins, Lara Couturier, Davis Jenkins, Rob Johnstone, Alison Kaldec, and Gretchen Schmidt. I have had the pleasure of working with this group for much of the last decade and, while there are many others who have contributed mightily to the completion movement, they have had a profound influence on me professionally and personally. I would be remiss if I didn't acknowledge these individuals. Thank you!

Thank you to my editors, Richard Alfred and Debbie Sydow. Their guidance and patience through this process have been phenomenal. More pointedly, I want to thank Dr. Alfred for the considerable impact he has had on my career. As a consultant to my former college, he encouraged me to apply for the higher education doctoral program at the University of Michigan. Once I was at U-M, he provided regular insight and direction as I navigated the program, and he was a thoughtful contributor to my dissertation committee. I'm gratified that he saw promise in my dissertation, which is the conceptual underpinning for this book. Thank you for your guidance and support.

Finally, and most importantly, I would like to thank my family for their constant love and inspiration as I wrote the manuscript. This project started shortly after I finished my doctorate, and I want to acknowledge their continued willingness to share their husband/dad with my life's work. My wife, Rachael, who is always very supportive, thought I was certifiable for taking on yet another big project. My children—Erin, Hannah, and Ben—wonder if their dad will ever not have to work at least part of a weekend. Thank you for ongoing support . . . and patience. I love you all very much!

Prologue

Equity and Quality in an Era of Completion

Community colleges—well known for providing an affordable access point for learners entering postsecondary education—are under significant pressure to improve student outcomes. Colleges and states are responding to growing evidence of the economic value of higher levels of credential attainment with a variety of innovations in policy and practice. This book will explore the benefits of increased educational attainment and the movement of states and colleges to respond to this evidence, but it will also investigate what may be lost—specifically, equity and quality—without thoughtful consideration of the choices made in a changing environment.

This prologue frames two debates that should be prominent in state capitols and on college campuses across the country, but are unfortunately muted or nonexistent. One of these issues centers on how colleges and states may reflexively limit access to students—many from underrepresented groups—because they are unprepared academically and are less likely to complete. The second debate focuses on the implications of increasing the number of postsecondary credentials without appropriate consideration of the labor market demand for them. The simple question that will be explored throughout this book is whether community colleges, government agencies, foundations, and others are adequately considering the negative consequences of actions stemming from the completion agenda.

PROTECTING EQUITY WHILE PROMOTING COMPLETION

The affordability of community colleges relative to other sectors of higher education has predictably led to a larger student population coming from lower-income backgrounds. Given the strong correlation between lower socioeconomic levels and minority racial/ethnic status, it is also not surprising that the affordability of community colleges results in a higher percentage of students enrolling in these institutions from underrepresented groups compared to four-year public and private universities. Given their open-access mission, community colleges also attract students that are the first generation in their families to enroll in postsecondary education. Taken together, these dynamics have established community colleges as uniquely accessible institutions for segments of the population that may not otherwise pursue education beyond high school. The issue of racial and economic stratification among the sectors of postsecondary education, while very important, is a different debate that will not be addressed here.

Looking back over several decades, the percentage of learners enrolled in postsecondary education has increased dramatically. This would not have been possible without community colleges playing the critical role of providing a low-cost, accessible option for millions of students. While this accomplishment should be celebrated, we must also understand that the accessibility gains of the past four decades are at risk. The threat emanates in part from the growing emphasis by policymakers and opinion leaders on student outcomes and degree attainment.

The completion agenda, which will be described in greater depth in chapter 1, is based on the premise that higher education institutions in general, but community colleges specifically, need to improve educational outcomes for our national and regional communities to be economically competitive. Community colleges have been the target of much of the attention of the completion agenda because their outcomes (as measured by graduation rates) have been dreadful compared to other sectors of higher education.

Acknowledging oft-cited shortcomings in the methodology the federal government uses for measuring community college student outcomes and setting aside the debate about what constitutes success, it should not be surprising that the graduation rates for students at two-year colleges are as low as they are. As noted earlier, these colleges attract disproportionately high numbers of first-generation, low-income, minority students, many of whom show up unprepared academically and facing other challenging noncognitive factors. Community college students arrive with a plethora of risk factors and 62 percent add to these factors by attending part-time because of other life circumstances.[1]

By painting a grim picture of the circumstances of those that attend community colleges, it is not the author's intent to attack the students or "blame the victim." Nor is the intent to provide an excuse for college faculty, staff, and leaders to avoid working aggressively to improve performance so more students can be successful. Rather, the goal is to remind the reader that the challenges many students face(d) were and are created by much larger societal dynamics than the colleges or their students can solve on their own. Policymakers and college leaders should avoid the urge to rush toward simple solutions to very complex issues. The gains in access of the past several decades can be undone if we do not collectively guard against solutions that undercut opportunity for the most at-risk populations. The next section identifies specific threats to equity and access in community colleges that could result from the completion agenda that will be addressed throughout this book.

The Challenge of College Readiness

Research has repeatedly documented that many students attending community colleges arrive considerably underprepared and with academic shortcomings. Depending on which study is cited, roughly 60 percent of students at community colleges are identified as needing developmental or remedial education in at least one subject. This number is derived from placement tests students take when enrolling at the colleges and doesn't reflect those that actually take a remedial course. Later chapters will explore strategies in use to reduce the number of students needing remediation and how students are assessed, as well as promising ways colleges and states are working to accelerate students that are not academically prepared through developmental courses. For now it is enough to say that there are examples of promising programs underway to address gaps in college readiness. However, there are also examples of fanciful solutions to this vexing issue that we should all be worried about.

Without going in depth into the history of developmental education, the concept emerged in the 1960s at a time when greater numbers of citizens made their way into postsecondary education. Not surprisingly, with larger enrollments, colleges began to see an increase in the number students who were not prepared for college-level work. Before this time, the general mindset was that students essentially had a "right to fail" and could take whatever courses they wanted without the institutions directing them. This approach was effective when primarily upper-class and upper-middle-class people were going to college and were more likely to be academically prepared. The need for developmental education was ushered in after World War II, when federal financial aid policy (for example, G. I. Bill, Pell Grant, etc.) created incentives for more people to attend college and an increasing number of the new students who enrolled were less prepared academically than their peers had been historically.

This trend resulted in substantial efforts to increase high school graduation standards and expectations—efforts that continue to this day in the form of the Common Core State Standards. It also led many colleges to initiate processes for assessment of student readiness at entry and placement in increasingly complex tiers of developmental courses in mathematics, reading, and / or writing. The process of remediation or developmental education has always been a core mission of community colleges, but it has become a controversial point within the completion agenda. The push to increase completion rates over the past decade has led to an exploration by states and colleges of the obstacles students encounter to progress and degree completion. Early on in this dialogue developmental education was identified as a significant barrier, and considerable resources were invested from national foundations, states, and colleges to confront the issue.

Much of the focus on reforming developmental education has centered on structural problems associated with remedial course sequences. These sequences were designed to place students at the appropriate content level based on test results, but they became a lightning rod in the push to improve student outcomes. Reform-minded critics rightly pointed to research that indicated students who had low placement test scores in math, for example, could end up spending multiple semesters in developmental courses with little or no chance of getting into a college-level course in the subject.[2] This research suggested that some students would succeed in the lower-level courses only to become frustrated with the long sequences and stop out before getting to college-level courses.

The evidence is fairly clear that the structure and delivery of developmental education can be a significant barrier for unprepared students, who disproportionately come from low-income and underrepresented backgrounds. Overall, tackling the development education issue is in itself an attempt to address equity issues, but unfortunately this is not where the story ends.

As stated earlier, the reasons for poor academic preparation are complex and intersect with broader social inequities that cannot be remedied simply by reforming developmental education. Unfortunately some states, which will be examined in later chapters, have adopted policies that fixate on developmental education—its structure, design, and delivery—as the problem and seek to eliminate the courses community colleges teach to remediate student deficiencies. Rather than attempting to reform developmental education in a way that would address the underlying challenge of college readiness, policymakers in some states have, to varying degrees, returned to the "right to fail" approach of forty-plus years ago.

This is an evolving story and a more thoughtful approach may win the day, but the implications of ill-considered policy prescriptions on equity and access should be clearly identified. If colleges do not have mechanisms in place to identify and help students that are academically unprepared, which can be particularly acute among minority populations, we will see a widening of the achievement and attainment gap on racial and economic lines.

Potential for Perverse Incentives Created
by Outcomes-Based Funding

Another potential threat to equity in higher education, and community colleges in particular, is the emergence of aggressive variants of performance-based funding that are focused squarely on educational attainment. Historically, funding for public colleges and universities has, in most states, been based on enrollments at the start of an academic year and/or term. In the past several years, there has been a marked shift toward funding that is based in part on how students are progressing toward and attaining a credential.

According to the National Conference of State Legislatures, by March 2015 thirty-two states had adopted formulas that allocate some portion of postsecondary funding based on "performance indicators such as course completion, time to degree, transfer rates, and the number of degrees awarded." Five others were transitioning to such a funding model.[3] Outcomes-based funding will be explored in greater detail in a later chapter, but it is important at this point to highlight the perverse incentives that outcomes-based funding models may create at open-access community colleges.

To respond to urgent calls for higher attainment rates, policymakers have focused on one of the few levers available to them to drive institutional behavior: funding. Setting aside the debate about the disinvestment in higher education by many states over the past decade, political leaders have legitimate concerns about whether their constituents are getting what they are paying for from postsecondary education institutions. Increasingly they point to low graduation rates as evidence that colleges and universities are falling short in their educational mission and are moving to change incentive structures that institutions are operating under by adopting outcomes-based funding formulas.

While newer formulas include components that reward institutions for graduating students from underrepresented groups, the overarching focus in most states is to prompt more students entering colleges and universities to complete a credential. As with the enrollment-oriented formulas that have been pervasive in the past, there is little doubt that institutions will respond to these new incentives and pursue strategies that boost completion—and by extension funding. The unanswered question is what these strategies will be. Will institutions begin to focus more intently on students that are more likely to succeed? By definition this approach could lead open-access community colleges to establish admissions criteria that have been largely nonexistent in the past.

Community college leaders are beginning to ask what institutions should do with learners who read at very low levels or can't do basic mathematics. These are not new issues, but the completion push is forc-ing community colleges to reconsider how to handle the population of students who are woefully underprepared academically. Some colleges have started to redirect students who place very low on math or English placement tests to other literacy programs provided by adult basic educa-tion (ABE) providers, thereby establishing a "floor" under which students cannot be admitted to the college. As institutions react to changing crite-ria for state funding, these issues will become acute, and it is possible that students at the lowest levels of preparation could be turned away.

Beyond the individual responses of colleges to changing funding realities, the collective reaction of colleges within states may also lead to problems related to equitable access. As the policy pressure around completion has become more pronounced and states have begun to create new accountability systems, which in many instances include outcome-based funding, metrics have been established to gauge insti-tutional performance. A key consideration for these metrics is what students should be counted in the cohorts that are tracked.

For example, in some states colleges and system offices have argued legitimately that students who are only coming for a few courses to en-hance their job skills should not be part of the cohort tracked for degree completion purposes. To operationalize this metric, some states have created cohort definitions that only include students after they success-fully complete twelve or fifteen credit hours, which equates to four or five courses. Again, the objective of this approach is to exclude those students who have no intention of completing an associate degree. The problem with this approach is that if it is not thoughtfully implemented, it could also exclude students who are academically unprepared, enroll in development education, and stop out before they reach the credit threshold to be included in the cohort. This accountability schema could make students that are not college ready practically invisible and lower the pressure on colleges to help this population succeed—a population that unfortunately too often includes disproportionally high percentages of low-income and minority students.

In the end one of the easiest ways for colleges to increase completion rates is to focus on students that are more likely to succeed and estab-lish higher admissions standards. As antithetical as this notion is to the historical open-access mission of community colleges, it is not without precedent. Less-selective universities have sought to brandish their repu-tations and enhance their standing as research institutions by increasing admissions standards and redirecting "less worthy" students to branch campuses or community colleges. The focus on degree completion at community colleges *could* lead two-year colleges to follow a similar path. The problem, of course, is that there is no reasonable option for community colleges to redirect unprepared students. If this scenario were to come to pass, community colleges would in effect close the open door and undermine equity access.

PRESERVING QUALITY WHILE ENHANCING OUTCOMES

In the latter half of the twentieth century, two-year institutions rightfully earned the moniker "community" college because of their responsiveness to local needs of citizens and employers. With strong connections to communities, colleges have also garnered sustained local support in return. Looking back several decades, a reputation for responsiveness has been fortified by colleges' ability and willingness to create new programs and offerings—credit and noncredit—designed to meet local labor market needs. This connection to community should be celebrated, but leaders must also understand that this defining characteristic of community colleges can be diminished unless it is thoughtfully protected. This challenge, like the threat to access, stems in part from the growing emphasis by policymakers and opinion leaders on student outcomes and degree attainment that may fundamentally change the way colleges operate.

The completion agenda is squarely focused on increasing the number of citizens with credentials, which by definition can devalue other aspects of the community college mission such as community service, contract training, and workforce development programming that tend to focus on noncredit (that is, nondegree) offerings. This is not to say that these functions don't lead to certificates or degrees, but transitions from noncredit to credit programs are inherently more difficult to track and quantify. Significant portions of the learners who show up at the doors of a community college enter through noncredit tracks. If policymakers and practitioners are not conscious of this, they run the risk of undermining a valued service the institutions provide to communities as well as a potential pipeline of students who could move to the credit side of a college and earn a credential.

There are more palpable threats to quality that could also emerge from the completion agenda. For one, as institutions seek to increase the number of credentials they award, they may in turn grant degrees with questionable labor market value. Alternatively, college faculty may feel added pressure to have more students progress and complete and inflate the grades students earn in individual classes, thereby decreasing the rigor of programs. Circumstances of this type are highly unlikely, but if policymakers, college leaders, and faculty do not guard against them, both are plausible. This is especially true as funding for colleges becomes more dependent on student outcomes. The next section will elaborate on the threats to program quality that could result from the completion agenda if adequate attention is not paid to issues of access and completion.

Reexamining the Potential for Perverse Incentives Created by Outcomes-Based Funding

With more states adopting outcomes-based funding, institutions are predictably looking for strategies to increase completion rates. As will be discussed in later chapters, some of these strategies include deep institution-wide reforms, while others are targeted interventions that are geared toward particular subsets of students. An example of a targeted approach would be efforts to zero in on students with some college but no degree as a means for reengaging these students and prompting them to reenroll and finish the credential they started. This is a perfectly legitimate strategy, and it makes sense to target students who were already working on a degree but dropped out. In fact, colleges (and states) are experimenting with policies and incentives to make it easier to target and attract this "near completer" population as one way to increase completion rates and meet attainment goals.[4]

As attractive as it is, this strategy can lead to problems if institutions restrict their focus to the number of students reengaged and awarded a degree without paying attention to the labor market value of the credential received. More specifically, some colleges employing these strategies have filtered eligible students through requirements for a general studies degree and awarded that credential and neglected the degree program the student intended to pursue. This is not to say the general studies degree is without value, but this approach suggests that colleges using this strategy are more concerned about the number of credentials awarded than the labor market impact for the students.

Another potentially troubling aspect of "near completer" strategies is the automatic awarding of degrees. Sometimes referred to as an "opt-out" approach, colleges contact students who are eligible for a degree and, unless students choose not to exercise this option, automatically award the credential. The idea of awarding a credential a student has earned is laudable, but to do so in a way that is not affirmed by the student may, in the long run, undermine the value of the credential in the labor market rather than strengthen it. If this happens, the degree could prove to be less helpful to the individual student. When using "near completer" strategies, it is important to ensure that appropriate precautions are in place to protect the quality of the credential. Without precautions, accusations could surface that community colleges are merely behaving as diploma mills, similar to the charges that have been levied against less-than-reputable for-profit institutions in the past.

Beyond the problems that could be posed by completion strategies, one of the most significant threats to quality stemming from the completion agenda is grade inflation. In a number of states that have adopted outcomes-based formulas, funding schemes include metrics not only of the number of credentials completed, but also intermediate milestones to gauge how students are progressing. An example of this metric is successful course completion. There is a considerable amount of research suggesting that credit accumulation thresholds are predictive of student success and completion.[5] Intermediate performance metrics and the funding tied to them are specifically designed to create incentives for institutions to focus on factors that will increase the number of students successfully meeting identified benchmarks. To accomplish this, the support of deans and department chairs will be necessary to reinforce the emphasis on completion benchmarks with faculty in academic disciplines.

As institutions, departments, and faculty are held accountable for intermediate outcomes and, by extension, funding implications, it is probable that colleges will make useful changes that will contribute to student success. It is plausible, however, that funding tied to these types of progression metrics will create perverse incentives that could lead instructors to take the easier path and simply reduce the rigor of courses and/or grading to help more students meet the benchmark. Perhaps most alarming about the potential negative effects of intermediate incentives is the fact that it is so difficult to detect and guard against grade inflation.

As was true with the discussion about equity, there is a relatively simple way for colleges to increase completion rates—decrease the rigor of programs and/or courses. On some level, it is human nature to follow the path of least resistance. If the pressure for improved outcomes is sufficiently high and the consequences for lower outcomes dire, instructors and staff may respond by making choices that could diminish the quality of course offerings. While these choices would be hard to detect or quantify, the larger impact on colleges over time could be substantial. If employers, some of whom already question the quality of skills delivered by higher education institutions, were to lose confidence in community colleges, their longstanding reputation for responsiveness could be irreparably damaged.

NOTES

1. "Fast Facts," *American Association of Community Colleges*, last modified February 2016, http://www.aacc.nche.edu/AboutCC/Pages/fastfactsfactsheet.aspx.

2. Thomas Bailey, Dong Wook Jeong, and Sung-Woo Cho, "Referral, Enrollment, and Completion in Developmental Education Sequences in Community Colleges," *Economics of Education Review* 29, no. 2 (2010): 255–70.

3. "Performance-Based Funding for Higher Education," *National Conference of State Legislatures,* last modified July 31, 2015, http://www.ncsl.org/research/education/performance-funding.aspx.

4. Clifford Adelman, *Searching for Our Lost Associate's Degrees: Project Win-Win at the Finish Line* (Washington, DC: Institute for Higher Education Policy, 2013).

5. Jeremy Offenstein, Colleen Moore, and Nancy Shulock, *Advancing by Degrees: A Framework for Increasing College Completion* (Washington, DC: The Institute for Higher Education Leadership and Policy and The Education Trust, 2010).

ONE

Confluence of Pressures

Economic and political forces have converged to push higher education institutions—especially community colleges—to improve student outcomes and boost education attainment. These forces include, but are not limited to, global economic competitiveness, rising tuition and decreased public subsidies, and the threat of displacement posed by emerging models for educational delivery. The pages that follow describe how these pressures have manifested in significant reform efforts promoted by state and national policymakers fueled by support and investment from national foundations. This discussion sets the context for challenges community colleges face as a result of the tension between access and completion in chapter 3 and a discussion of the thrust of the completion agenda in chapter 4.

PUTTING THE COMPLETION AGENDA IN CONTEXT

Community colleges have served as an important entry point for millions of students who otherwise may not have enrolled in postsecondary education. When measured by increased enrollment over the past several decades, the effectiveness of community colleges is nothing short of extraordinary. Between 1963 and 2006, public two-year college enrollments increased by 667 percent from approximately 740,000 students in 1963 to more than 6.2 million students in 2006.[1] However, when the lens of effectiveness shifts to student outcomes—namely, the completion of a credential—community colleges have considerable room for improvement, with only 22.5 percent of students attending public two-year colleges nationally graduating within three years.[2]

Before delving into the specifics of the completion agenda, it is important to first understand the factors that have contributed to its emergence. The underlying dynamic is a changing domestic economy and increased global competition. Economic realities have reinforced the

1

belief that at least some education beyond high school is required for individuals to find family-sustaining employment and realize a reasonable quality of life. Analyses by researchers at Georgetown University buttress this point, suggesting that more than 60 percent of all jobs will require some postsecondary education and many will require at least an associate degree by 2018.[3] When these projections are compared to current levels of educational attainment, the impetus behind the completion agenda becomes clear.

The most recent report from the Lumina Foundation, *A Stronger Nation through Higher Education*, states that over 61 percent of adults age twenty-five to sixty-four have some college. However, further study of these numbers indicates that 22 percent of adults age twenty-five to sixty-four have some college but no degree.[4] On the surface this would appear to be a promising indicator of engagement in postsecondary education, but much of the literature suggests that individuals only realize the benefits of higher education if they attain a credential, not just attend college.

A closer examination of the percentage of adults with degrees points to the primary reason the focus on degree completion in community colleges has been particularly intense. Overall, the proportion of adults (twenty-five to sixty-four years old) with any postsecondary degrees is 39.4 percent. Of this population, only 8.7 percent hold an associate degree. While community college advocates legitimately point to alternative sub-baccalaureate outcomes (for example, workforce training and transfer) as being largely absent in these data, the low percentage of completers is stark when one considers that nearly half of all undergraduates now enroll in community colleges.[5]

To draw out the distinction between two- and four-year public institutions further, it is useful to compare graduation rates for public community college and universities collected by the U.S. Department of Education. These data reflect the percentage of first-time, full-time students who graduate within 150 percent of normal time. For two-year institutions, 150 percent of normal time is three years. This compares to six years for four-year institutions. The graduation rate in public community colleges is 19 percent nationally compared to 55 percent for public universities.[6] Low graduation rates have directly resulted in increased calls for improvement across all higher education institutions. While there are legitimate reasons why community college rates are low as well as valid critiques about how federal graduation rates are calculated, the focus on the two-year sector has been particularly intense for obvious reasons.

With this data as a backdrop, we can turn to the origin and evolution of the "completion agenda" over the last decade. It is difficult to isolate a single event that led to the increased focus on educational attainment, but the publication of a national best seller—*The World Is Flat*—followed closely by the release of a U.S. Department of Education "Spellings Commission" report—*A Test of Leadership: Charting the Future of U.S. Higher Education*—crystalized opinion leaders' views of the waning position of the United States in terms of global economic competitiveness and educational achievement.[7] While neither publication focused solely on increasing degree attainment, both pointed to an alarming stagnation in U.S. educational attainment compared to emerging economies in China and India and the implications of this trend for national economic competitiveness.

Other lesser-known reports from organizations such as the National Academies of Science and the Organization for Economic Co-operation and Development confirmed what mainstream prognosticators were saying: if the United States does not increase the educational attainment of its citizens, the country would fall behind economically and Americans' standard of living would decline.[8] The alarms sounded in the last decade were magnified considerably by the great recession that began in 2008.

PLETHORA OF COMPLETION INITIATIVES EMERGE

In the years immediately following these publications, state policymakers, national higher education associations, and other advocacy groups began to adopt a more aggressive stance toward college completion by pushing goals to increase educational attainment.[9] These diverse and often disconnected efforts were catalyzed by the investments of several major foundations and advocacy for increased educational attainment by the Obama administration.

While substantial funding to support completion initiatives was already in place from the philanthropic community, the completion agenda was powerfully reinforced when President Barack Obama embraced college completion early in his administration. The president set two goals for educational attainment: "by 2020, America will once again have the highest proportion of college graduates in the world, and community colleges will produce an additional 5 million graduates."[10] The Obama administration did not view the completion agenda as an end in itself—increased education attainment was critical not only for addressing the country's slipping economic position globally, but also for supporting the economic recovery from the deep recession.

To this end, the president proposed the American Graduation Initiative (AGI) in July 2009, which called for an investment of $12 billion over ten years to support community colleges and the completion goals in AGI. On the heels of AGI, President Obama also called for greater transparency of outcomes in the form of a ratings system for higher education institutions, launched programs and hosted a series of high-profile gatherings focused on supporting students from low-income and unrepresented groups, and most recently announced an aggressive strategy to provide a free community college education for anyone who wants it. While funding for the AGI was eventually scaled back to $2 billion and debate continued about other aspects of the president's agenda for college completion, the Obama administration signaled an unprecedented commitment to community colleges coupled with a belief that two-year institutions were critical to achieving national educational attainment goals.

Reinforcing the president's call for increased completion rates, a number of foundations working with an alphabet soup of intermediaries sought to create a platform for reform in the field. Table 1.1 highlights some of the major national initiatives that have emerged in the past decade to promote increased college completion. It is important to note that most of these initiatives were focused squarely on community colleges. The Bill and Melinda Gates Foundation and the Lumina Foundation for Education have been the primary funders of most of these initiatives, but they have also partnered with the Carnegie Corporation of New York, the Ford Foundation, and the Kresge Foundation—organizations that have made substantial investments in community college education.[11]

While operating features of the initiatives in this table will be explored in later chapters, it is useful at this point to highlight the broad concepts underlying these and other initiatives not included in the table. Most of these initiatives sought to impact student outcomes by operating at multiple levels, with some focusing on specific groups of students and/or interventions at individual colleges and others emphasizing broader institutional change. Still others operate at the state level attempting to create policy conditions that would be more conducive to increased credential attainment. Some of the more elaborate efforts sought to spur action at multiple levels simultaneously. Arguably the most influential of these initiatives in the community college sector has been Achieving the Dream (ATD).

ATD was launched in 2004 with twenty-eight colleges in five states through substantial investment from the Lumina Foundation. It was designed to foster institution-wide change while aggressively promoting needed state policy reforms and stimulating deep research to determine what was actually happening to community college students. The ATD network has since grown to over two hundred colleges in thirty-five states with financial support and technical assistance from dozens of local, state, and national partners and funders.[12] At the time ATD was established, most colleges were focused on how many students entered their institutions with little emphasis on what happened after the start of a new academic year.

The policy focus of most states for community colleges was on buildings and budgets. In the ten years since it was launched, ATD has served

Table 1.1.   Major U.S. College Completion Initiatives

Initiative	Goal	Year Launched
Achieving the Dream	To help more community college students, particularly low-income students and students of color, stay in school and earn a college certificate or degree.	2004
Access to Success	To cut the college-going and graduation gaps for low-income and minority students in half by 2015.	2007
College Completion Agenda	To increase the proportion of twenty-five to thirty-four year olds who hold an associate degree or higher to 55 percent by the year 2025 in order to make American a leader in education attainment in the world.	2008
College Completion Initiative	To significantly increase the number of students who complete career certificates and associate's and bachelor's degrees so that 60 percent of each state's adults age twenty-five to sixty-four will have one of these credentials by 2025.	2008
Adult College Completion Network	To unite organizations and agencies working to increase college completion by adults with prior credits but no degree in a collaborative learning network.	2010
College Completion Challenge	To promote the development and implementation of policies, practices, and institutional cultures that will produce 50 percent more students with high-quality degrees and certificates by 2020, while increasing access and quality.	2010
Complete College America	To significantly increase the number of Americans with a college degree or credential of value and to close attainment gaps for traditionally underrepresented populations.	2010
Complete to Compete	To raise national awareness about the need to increase college completion and productivity, create a set of common higher education completion and productivity measures, develop a series of best practices and a list of policy actions to increase college completion, provide grants to states to design policies and programs that increase college completion, and hold a learning institute for key advisors on successful strategies to graduate more students.	2010
Ensuring America's Future by Increasing Latino College Completion	To inform, engage, and sustain efforts to promote the role of Latinos in making the United States the work leader in college degree completion.	2010
ACE Commission on Education Attainment	To assess the needed for improved college retention and attainment and to chart a course for improvement.	2011
Boosting College Completion in a New Economy	To work with legislative and higher education leaders to improve their state economies by increasing the number of residents with a postsecondary credential.	2011

Source: Adapted from American Association of State Colleges and Universities. Alene Russell, *A Guide to Major U.S. College Completion Initiatives* (Washington, DC: American Association of State Colleges and Universities, 2010).

as clarion call for change in community colleges nationally. Many of the initiatives outlined in table 1.1 are in some part related to ATD and reflect the increasing sophistication of the national dialogue around the completion agenda. Following are brief descriptions of some of the key elements that have been the focus of completion initiatives over the past decade.

Institution-Wide Reform Efforts

With ATD leading the way, a number of initiatives have employed a broad approach to influencing the way colleges operate. Completion by Design, funded by the Gates Foundation, is, as the name implies, geared toward pushing colleges to rethink how they interact with students from the moment of initial connection before they enroll through completion of a credential with labor market value and/or further education. This initiative is structured around a "loss/momentum framework" that identifies both the points at which students stop out of college and the opportunities where institutions can build momentum to keep students on track. This work, which focused on colleges in Florida, North Carolina, and Ohio, is the foundation of an important dialogue emerging nationally about the need for guided or structured pathways. The idea is to move students into clear programs of study faster and ensure they have adequate monitoring and support to stay on a path toward completion.

The work of the Center for Community College Student Engagement (CCCSE) based at the University of Texas at Austin has also played a critical role in promoting institution-wide reforms contributing to student success. Through a series of surveys routinely conducted at colleges across the country, CCCSE has developed a substantial understanding from the perspectives of faculty, staff, and most importantly students about practices that make a difference in student success. This work culminated in the 2014 publication *A Matter of Degrees: Practices to Pathways*, a report presenting key findings from a multiyear CCCSE initiative to identify high-impact educational practices in community colleges.[13]

Enhancing Data Availability, Use, and Transparency

One of the important legacies of ATD has been its influence on increased use of data in decisions about strategies to improve student outcomes. For participating colleges and states, ATD has instilled a culture of evidence that heretofore had been lacking. A decade ago, many community colleges had little or no institutional research capacity, and for those that had capacity the primary focus was on compliance reporting. ATD began to change this culture by pushing colleges to dig deeper into what was happening to students, understanding when they were dropping out, and using this information to design retention interventions. Institutional research capacity is still a problem for many colleges as external reporting requirements continue to grow, but ATD has been a formidable force in changing the approach to analytics and their use in decisions.

Completion initiatives have helped define what is meant by student success. While the debate about a definition of student success continues, initiatives like ATD have sidestepped this controversy by describing student success as the completion of a credential with labor market value and/or the successful continuation of education (that is, transfer). Using this description, states and colleges have been able to focus on clear categories of outcomes. Remaining, however, is important work to develop a set of metrics that can help practitioners and policymakers understand how students progress and succeed.

An important example of this work is the American Association of Community Colleges's Voluntary Framework of Accountability (VFA). The VFA is designed as a parsimonious set of metrics that accurately reflect the unique mission and student population of community colleges. It is one of several efforts to develop a set of performance measures to track student progress and success. The College Board established the Completion Arch in an attempt to bring coherence to multiple initiatives for gauging student outcomes (for example, Complete College America and the National Governors Association), but all share a common objective: to create clear and transparent performance indicators at the national, state, and local levels.

Reforming Developmental Education and Improving College Readiness

As noted in the prologue, the number of students requiring developmental education at community colleges and the limited success of students progressing from remediation into college-level courses has spurred a considerable amount of attention as part of the completion agenda. Research indicates that a major problem with developmental education is the long sequence of remedial courses that students must take if they have substantial academic deficiencies.[14] Unfortunately, too many students that place in these sequences never complete all of the courses in the sequence and stop out before entry into college-level courses required for the degree. Another problem with developmental education has been assessment strategies used to determine the level of student academic preparation, as well of the process colleges use to administer assessments for placing students in courses.

A number of national initiatives have focused on reforming developmental education. The Developmental Education Initiative funded by the

Gates Foundation was built directly on ATD and has pushed colleges and states to develop practices and policies that would move students faster to and through gatekeeper courses. Based on this work, several states and institutions have embarked on efforts to create shorter modules of content targeted toward learner deficiencies. This initiative has also resulted in the development of new assessment strategies, some of which have been used in partnership with high schools to gauge students' level of readiness in their junior year and to remediate deficiencies in their senior year of high school.

There have been a number of initiatives and projects geared toward accelerating students' progress through developmental education. One exemple is the Accelerated Learning Program, a co-requisite model for developmental writing pioneered at the Community College of Baltimore County that pairs a college-level writing class with the developmental writing class and delivers supplemental instruction to students. Another area of significant work has focused on clarifying college-level math that students need for different academic programs and streamlining the path for remediation of deficiencies. The Carnegie Foundation for the Advancement of Teaching's Quantway and Statway projects and the New Mathways Project at the Charles A. Dana Center at the University of Texas at Austin are two of the most prominent and promising initiatives in this area.

It is important to note that there have also been substantial efforts to improve college readiness for students coming directly out of high school. The progress toward improving college readiness certainly predates the completion agenda, with many states increasing the rigor of their curriculum and their assessment of secondary students in the 1990s. However, in the past decade individual state efforts have been eclipsed by the national effort led by the Council of Chief State School Officers and National Governors Association to establish Common Core State Standards. While the implementation of these standards and related assessments has been the subject of considerable controversy, the underlying idea is that if states and institutions want to see more students complete a college degree, it will be necessary to ensure that they are ready for college-level work when they arrive.

Targeting Adults with or without Some College

While the completion agenda is not exclusively geared toward traditional-age students, much of the framing for reforms has been through the lens of student progression through the educational pipeline. As a result, the dialogue in many states, which has been reinforced by initiatives like Achieving the Dream and Completion by Design, has been biased toward students directly out of high school. That said, there have also been a number of initiatives focused on adults returning to college and/ or to address the challenges of adults with marginal basic skills. One of the first initiatives to emerge as part of the completion agenda in 2003 was Bridges to Opportunity. This project, funded by the Ford Foundation, was designed to bring about changes in state policy and community college practice to promote educational opportunities for low-income adults.

Bridges to Opportunity was the precursor to two larger efforts targeting the same population—Breaking Through and Accelerating Opportunity. Breaking Through was focused on helping colleges advance low-skill adults into careers through strategies that accelerate learning, provide comprehensive supports, and incorporate course content with a labor market payoff. A key challenge identified through both Bridges to Opportunity and Breaking Through was the misalignment of systems to support adults with low basic skills. The Accelerating Opportunity initiative emerged to address this issue and sought to change the delivery of Adult Basic Education (ABE) by integrating basic skills education and credit-bearing career technical/occupational programs with clear connections to employment. The goal of this ongoing work was to make ABE an on ramp for adult student entry and completion of postsecondary education.

In addition to efforts targeting adults with low basic skills, there have also been a number of initiatives that have sought to encourage adults with some college but no degree to reenroll and finish the credential they started. In many states, this "some college" population represents a significant number of adults and is an opportunity for policymakers and practitioners to help learners reach completion and attainment goals. According to the most recent edition of the Lumina Foundation's *Stronger Nation through Higher Education* report, 22 percent or 36 million adults between ages twenty-five and sixty-four have some college but no degree. Not surprisingly, the Lumina Foundation and other organizations have been particularly aggressive in pursuing strategies that target this group.

An illustration of this work is the Adult College Completion Network, which was funded by the Lumina Foundation and managed by the Western Interstate Commission for Higher Education. This is a collaborative learning network of organizations and agencies across the country working to increase college completion by adults with prior college credits but no degree. Two initiatives in this area that have received substantial attention are Project Win-Win and Credit When It's Due.

Project Win-Win targets students who have accumulated a considerable number of credits but are no longer enrolled at any institution and have not received a credential. The intent is to encourage these students to return to college and complete the limited number of requirements needed to complete a degree. Credit When It's Due is focused on students who transferred to a university prior to completing an associate degree. The objective of this initiative is to encourage students to "reverse transfer" credits to the community college that will satisfy outstanding degree requirements so they can be retroactively awarded the associate degree. These national initiatives have been playing out in a variety of ways in state and local institutions as policymakers and practitioners look for easier ways to increase attainment levels by going after students who have already made considerable progress.

Focus on Underrepresented Groups and Nonacademic Risk Factors

Nearly all the national completion initiatives in the past decade have had a stated or implicit goal of improving the outcomes of students from underrepresented groups. Driven by achievement gaps that begin in primary and secondary education and extend to colleges and universities, national organizations and their large foundation benefactors have sought to support equity and social justice aspects of the completion agenda by also funding specific initiatives targeting underprivileged groups.

Examples of these initiatives are the Roadmap for Ensuring America's Future by Increasing Latino College Completion through Excelencia in Education, the Center for Community College Student Engagement's dual initiatives Improving Outcomes for Men of Color in Community Colleges and Engaging Latino Students for Transfer and College Completion and the Minority-Serving Institutions Models of Success Program managed by the Institute for Higher Education Policy. These initiatives are focused on working with individual institutions to improve programming for specific subgroups of students. In most cases, the interventions promoted through these efforts emulate the broad set of best practices to support student completion on a nation-wide scale.

Beyond programs that target specific subgroups are a number of initiatives that have sought to address nonacademic factors like housing, childcare, transportation, and other life issues that too often interfere with degree completion. Programs such as Benefits Access for College Completion have worked with colleges to develop practices that connect low-income students to an array of public benefits, such as food assistance and health insurance. Similarly, the Working Family Student Success Network seeks to help low-income families achieve financial stability by extending public benefits beyond traditional financial support through career advising and financial literacy.

Influencing Institutional Leaders and Awarding Prizes
for Excellence

Foundations have sought to influence major national associations to embrace and support the completion agenda. For example, AACC, ACCT, and several other national community college organizations came together in 2010 in response to the pressure from policymakers and foundations to announce the College Completion Challenge. This challenge pledges to increase student completion rates by 50 percent over the next decade.[15]

In 2011 AACC launched the 21st-Century Initiative, with an explicit goal of increasing the total number of students with credentials by five million by 2020. This work, which was funded by the Gates and Kresge Foundations along with ACT and the Education Testing Service, culminated in the publication of *Reclaiming the American Dream: Community Colleges and the Nation's Future.*[16] This report was unusually blunt in its critique of community colleges and called for a redesign of students' educational experiences, a reinvention of institutional roles, and a reset of the entire system to improve student outcomes.

Parallel to the work of AACC, ACCT has worked to educate its membership—community college trustees—through a professional development series called Governance Institute for Student Success. Historically, boards of trustees have focused on college finances, capital projects, human resources, and program approvals. The Governance Institute is designed to elevate the issue of student success to help trustees assess a board's readiness to advance a student success agenda, to enhance awareness of the data needed to make decisions pertaining to student progress and completion, to strengthen governance practices in support of student completion, and to promote completion as a key element of institutional performance.

The Aspen Institute, in partnership with Achieving the Dream, has focused on leadership development as a critical component of the completion agenda. Building on lessons learned as part of the Aspen Prize for Community College Excellence, the Aspen Institute has developed Tools to Hire Exceptional Community College Presidents to assist college trustees in hiring CEOs with skills that will help them advance a student success agenda on their campus. Recognizing the impending retirement of a substantial number of current community college presidents, the Aspen Institute has also developed a curriculum for community college staff that aspires to senior leadership positions.[17]

In addition to investing in specific initiatives targeting leaders of community colleges and national associations, foundations have also funded a number of high-profile awards to shape field and public opinion about what is needed to improve completion rates in two-year colleges. Two of the most prominent examples are the Aspen Prize for Community College Excellence and the Talent Dividend Prize managed by CEOs for Cities.

The Aspen Prize is $1 million awarded to a community college every two years for excellence in relation to student outcomes and completion. This prize focuses on student learning, certificate and degree completion, employment and earnings, and access and success for minority and low-income students. The Talent Dividend is also a $1 million prize awarded to the city that exhibits the greatest increase in the number of postsecondary degrees granted over a four-year period. While investments from foundations for these prizes are fairly modest, the effect on the field is dramatic and has been a catalyst for action by individual institutions and metropolitan areas.

Shaping Public Policy

Foundations have funded multipronged initiatives to not only push for change at the institutional level, but also to influence policymakers. The emphasis on completion of the Obama administration and numerous philanthropic efforts have evolved in parallel with the efforts of state policymakers to enact policy changes geared toward creating conditions for improved completion rates.

Summarizing the policy reforms in numerous states, the College Completion Toolkit created by the U.S. Department of Education articulated seven strategies governors should consider when promoting college completion: 1) set goals and develop an action plan; 2) embrace performance-based funding; 3) align high school standards with college entrance and placement standards; 4) make transfer easier for students; 5) use data to drive decision making; 6) accelerate learning and reduce costs; and 7) target adults, especially those with some college but no degree.[18]

Efforts to encourage states to adopt these policies have been undertaken with membership organizations of elected state political leaders such as the National Governors Association and the National Conference of State Legislatures and as political appointees by the State Higher Education Executive Officers Association.

These strategies will be explored in more detail in chapter 4, but it is important to note that there have been several national initiatives geared toward changing state policies related to student progression and completion. The longest running of these efforts is the Postsecondary State Policy Network, which has been managed by Jobs for the Future as part of Achieving the Dream for the past twelve years. This network has involved ongoing deep work with state system offices, boards of higher education, and community college associations in fifteen states focused on policy levers similar to those in the College Completion Toolkit.

In 2009 several foundations funded the creation of Complete College America with many of the same policy objectives. This organization has worked to directly influence governors and legislators in thirty-five states and taken an aggressive stance to push colleges to improve outcomes.

The Lumina Foundation has created Strategy Labs as part of its overarching goal to increase educational attainment. Strategy Labs are an open platform for leaders and policymakers in all fifty states to come together to share research, data, and professional experience to advance Lumina's Goal 2025 to increase the proportion of Americans with high-quality college degrees, certificates, or other credentials to 60 percent by 2025. The thrust focuses on three core elements—improve student outcomes, align investments, and create smarter pathways.

The synergetic relationship between higher education policymakers—at both the state and federal levels—and the philanthropic community is indicative of an aggressive foundation role that has been labeled "advocacy philanthropy."[19] A 2013 analysis by the *Chronicle of Higher Education* highlights the influential role the philanthropic community has played in promoting degree completion with three foundations—the Bill and Melinda Gates Foundation, the Lumina Foundation for Education, and the Kresge Foundation—providing a half-billion dollars over the past decade to support large-scale reform initiatives.[20]

Contesting the Definition of Student Success a Decade into the Completion Agenda

As community colleges grapple with the completion agenda, it is important to understand that the definition of student success is subject to multiple interpretations. For the purposes of this book, student success is defined as the completion of a certificate or degree and/or successful transfer to a four-year institution. This definition is borrowed from Achieving the Dream and is reflective of the goals of the national initiatives outlined earlier.

While a clear definition of student success is useful as a vehicle for reform, critics suggest that such definitions are too narrow when considering the scope and mission of community colleges and the intentions of students.[21] Students enroll in community colleges for a variety of reasons, including career preparation, transfer to a four-year institution, skill upgrading and career change, and personal enrichment.

It is also true that some students enter college with no intention of earning a credential.[22] One of the most frequently cited reasons by practitioners for community college students not attaining a credential is that they had no intention of doing so from the start. Consequently, it is appropriate to take student intentions into account when considering outcomes. If students' aspirations are, in fact, to take a few courses to upgrade their skills or to transfer to a university, colleges should not be penalized for those that do not complete a degree.[23]

In a study that sought to create a typology of community college students, six distinctive clusters of student behavior were identified: transfer, vocational, drop-in, noncredit, experimental, and exploratory.[24] This study extends previous attempts to categorize community college students using rigorous cluster analysis over a seven-year period to track student enrollment and course-taking patterns in California. The result provides a clearer picture of how students use community colleges, which supports the notion that not all students enroll looking for a credential.[25]

As calls for improving outcomes grow louder, clarity will need to be achieved in relation to student educational goals, and more sophisticated methodologies for measuring success will also be necessary. Based on a study by the National Center for Education Statistics, we know that approximately 90 percent of students who enroll in community colleges intend to earn a credential.[26] This study also found that only 51 percent of the students enrolled with a goal of garnering a degree or certificate or transferring to a four-year institution actually did so. There is little question that a significant number of students entering community colleges with the intent of earning a credential are unable to do so. If colleges are to realize improvement in student outcomes, it is important to understand the reasons why students leave college short of a degree or certificate.

Another often cited factor that contributes to low completion rates is the number of students requiring remediation before they can move into college-level coursework. As noted in the prologue, college readiness is a major national issue, and the burgeoning need for and scope of developmental education is one of the most intractable problems facing community college practitioners. Bailey, Jeong, and Cho's recent study of developmental education points to research that suggests that between 43 and nearly 60 percent of all entering community college students nationally require at least one remedial course.[27]

Other challenges to the definition of student success include what critics describe as flawed performance metrics related to student outcomes. The argument is that the graduation rate as calculated by the U.S. Department of Education through the Graduation Rate Survey is inadequate because part-time students, who make up a large percentage of community college enrollments, are excluded. Further, the federal approach to measuring graduation rates does not include students who successfully transfer to four-year colleges as an accomplishment for community colleges, despite the fact that transfer is a core mission of two-year institutions and the intent of substantial number of entering students.[28]

The good news is that efforts are ongoing to improve the metrics used to gauge student progression and success.[29] The bad news is that improved metrics that more accurately reflect the community college student population will continue to demonstrate a significant gap between the number of students completing credentials and the projected labor market demand for individuals with more education.[30] It is this gap that is driving policymakers and foundations to focus on improving student outcomes and evidence of increased educational attainment.

NOTES

1. Stephen Provasnik and Michael Planty, *Community Colleges: Special Supplement to the Condition of Education 2008* (Washington, DC: National Center for Education Statistics, 2008).

2. Laura G. Knapp, Janice E. Kelly-Reid, and Scott A. Ginder, *Enrollment in Postsecondary Institutions, Fall 2010; Financial Statistics, Fiscal Year 2010; and Graduation Rates, Selected Cohorts, 2002–07* [NCES 2012-280] (Washington, DC: National Center for Education Statistics, 2012).

3. Anthony P. Carnevale, Nicole Smith, and Jeff Stohl, *Help Wanted: Projections of Jobs and Education Requirements through 2018* (Washington DC: Georgetown University, Center on Education and the Workforce, 2010).

4. Lumina Foundation, *A Stronger Nation 2016* (Indianapolis, IN: Lumina Foundation, 2016).

5. Provasnik and Planty, *Community Colleges.*

6. U.S. Department of Education, National Center for Education Statistics, Integrated Postsecondary Education Data System (IPEDS), Winter 2014–15 Graduation Rates Component (*Digest of Education Statistics 2015*, table 326.10 and table 326.20).

7. Thomas L. Friedman, *The World Is Flat: A Brief History of the Twenty-First Century* (New York: Farrar, Straus and Giroux, 2005); U.S. Department of Education, *A Test of Leadership: Charting the Future of U.S. Higher Education* (Washington, DC: U.S. Department of Education, 2006).

8. National Academies of Science, *Rising Above the Gathering Storm: Energizing and Employing America for a Brighter Economic Future* (Washington, DC: National Academies of Science, 2005); Organisation for Economic Co-operation and Development, *Education at a Glance 2005: OECD Indicators* (OECD Publishing, 2005).

9. Michael L. Collins, *By the Numbers: State Goals for Increasing Postsecondary Attainment* (Boston: Jobs for the Future, 2006); Kevin J. Dougherty and Monica Reid Kerrigan, *Fifty States of Achieving the Dream: State Policies to Enhance Access to and Success in Community Colleges across the United States* (New York: Community College Research Center, 2007).

10. President Barack Obama, *Investing in Education: The American Graduation Initiative* (Washington, DC: The White House, 2009).

11. Alene Russell, *A Guide to Major U.S. College Completion Initiatives* (Washington, DC: American Association of State Colleges and Universities, 2010).

12. Achieving the Dream, *History* (Silver Spring, MD: Achieving the Dream), accessed October 1, 2016, http://www.achievingthedream.org/about-us/history.

13. Center for Community College Student Engagement, *A Matter of Degrees: Practices to Pathways* (Austin, TX: Center for Community College Student Engagement, The University of Texas at Austin, 2014).

14. Thomas Bailey, Dong Wook Jeong, and Sung-Woo Cho, "Referral, Enrollment, and Completion in Developmental Education Sequences in Community Colleges," *Economics of Education Review* 29, no. 2 (2010): 255–70.

15. American Association of Community Colleges, *College Completion Challenge: A Call to Action* (Washington, DC: American Association of Community Colleges, 2012).

16. 21st-Century Commission on the Future of Community Colleges, *Reclaiming the American Dream: Community Colleges and the Nation's Future* (Washington, DC: American Association of Community Colleges, 2012).

17. Aspen Institute College Excellence Program, *Hiring Exceptional Community College Presidents: Tools for Hiring Leaders Who Advance Student Access and Success* (Washington, DC: Aspen Institute, 2014).

18. U.S. Department of Education, *College Completion Toolkit* (Washington, DC: U.S. Department of Education, 2010).

19. Cassie Hall and Scott L. Thomas, "'Advocacy Philanthropy' and the Public Policy Agenda: The Role of Modern Foundations in American Higher Education," 93rd Annual Meeting of the American Educational Research Association, Vancouver, Canada, 2012.

20. Marc Perry, Kelly Field, and Beckie Supiano, "The Gates Effect," *Chronicle of Higher Education*, July 19, 2013.

21. Debra D. Bragg, "Community College Access, Mission, and Outcomes: Considering Intriguing Intersections and Challenges," *Peabody Journal of Education* 76, no. 1 (2001): 93–116; Arthur M. Cohen and Florence B. Brawer, *The American Community College*, fifth edition (San Francisco: Jossey-Bass Publishers, 2008).

22. Cohen and Brawer, *The American Community College*.

23. Thomas Bailey, Davis Jenkins, and Timothy Leinbach, *Is Student Success Labeled Institutional Failure? Student Goals and Graduation Rates in the Accountability Debate at Community Colleges* (New York: Community College Research Center, Teachers College, Columbia University, 2005); Bragg, "Community College Access, Mission, and Outcomes"; Juan Carlos Calcagno, Thomas Bailey, Davis Jenkins, Gregory Kienzl, and Timothy Leinbach, "Community College Student Success: What Institutional Characteristics Make a Difference?" *Economics of Education Review* 27 (2008): 632–45; Willard C. Hom, "The Denominator as the 'Target,'" *Community College Review* 37 (2009): 136–52.

24. Peter Bahr, "The Bird's Eye View of Community Colleges: A Behavioral Typology of First-Time Students Based on Cluster Analytic Classification," *Research in Higher Education* 51 (2010): 724–49.

25. Hom, "The Denominator as the 'Target'"; Laura Horn and Thomas Weko, *On Track to Complete? A Taxonomy of Beginning Community College Students and Their Outcomes 3 Years after Enrolling: 2003–04 through 2006* (Washington, DC: National

Center for Education Statistics, 2009); Stephen G. Katsinas, "Two-Year College Classifications Based on Institutional Control, Geography, Governance, and Size," *New Directions for Community Colleges* 122 (2003): 17–28; Jamie P. Merisotis and Jessica M. Shedd, "Using IPEDS to Develop a Classification System for Two-Year Postsecondary Institutions," *New Directions for Community Colleges* 122 (2003): 47–61.

26. Gary Hoachlander and C. Dennis Carroll, *Community College Students: Goals, Academic Preparation, and Outcomes* (Washington, DC: National Center for Education Statistics, 2003).

27. Bailey, Jeong, and Cho, "Referral, Enrollment, and Completion in Developmental Education Sequences in Community Colleges."

28. Thomas Bailey, Juan Carlos Calcagno, Davis Jenkins, Timothy Leinbach, and Gregory Kienzl, "Is Student-Right-To-Know All You Should Know? An Analysis of Community College Graduation Rates," *Research in Higher Education* 47, no. 5 (2006): 491–519; Christopher Baldwin, Estela Mara Bensimon, Alicia Dowd, and Lisa Klieman, "Measuring Student Success," *New Directions for Community Colleges* 153 (2011): 75–88.

29. Committee on Measures of Student Success, *A Report to Secretary of Education Arne Duncan* (Washington, DC: U.S. Department of Education, 2011); Kent Phillippe, *Voluntary Framework of Accountability: Metrics Manual Version 4.1* (Washington, DC: American Association of Community Colleges, 2016).

30. Carnevale, Smith, and Stohl, *Help Wanted: Projections of Jobs and Education Requirements through 2018.*

TWO

Competing Logics for Community Colleges

To better understand how the shifts in external expectations are impacting community colleges, this chapter explores the tension between access and completion through the lens of competing institutional logics. Institutional logics are the formal and informal rules of action, interaction, and interpretation that guide and constrain decisionmakers in pursuing an organization's mission and goals.

The concept of competing institutional logics is useful for understanding divergent beliefs and practices implicit in the shifting emphasis from access to success for community college students. This chapter will first explore the theoretical origins of logics, which are derived from the larger body of literature in institutional theory. Next it will explore the defining characteristics of institutional logics, including their influence on individual and organizational action, the multilevel manner in which they operate, and the means by which logics change and evolve.

Using concrete examples, the competing logics framework is used to illuminate how community colleges adjust to a different set of rules and practices to support completion and how these rules and practices contrast with, and in some instances contradict, the historical emphasis on access.

THEORETICAL FOUNDATION OF LOGICS

The concept of logics emerged from institutional theory in the 1970s and 1980s, which emphasized the importance of the external environment in shaping organizational expectations that, in turn, are reflected in formal practices, structures, and characteristics of organizations.

Leading scholars in institutional theory Meyer and Rowan suggested that embedded in the formal structure of organizations are myths that are ceremoniously adopted to placate external expectations. These myths are decoupled from the core functions of an organization to shield it from rigorous (and unwanted) assessments of performance. Organizations

19

in highly institutionalized environments further avoid risk by copying the behavior of industry peers.[1] This is known as isomorphism, a term coined by DiMaggio and Powell in work suggesting that three types of isomorphism—coercive, mimetic, and normative—lead organizations to become more similar over time in their search for legitimacy.[2] Overall, the emphasis of both Meyer and Rowan and DiMaggio and Powell was on organizational legitimacy and the ways in which organizational structures become more similar.

Brint and Karabel related the work of institutional theory scholars to community colleges by drawing parallels between the formal structure of American community colleges and concepts espoused by institutional theory. Using Meyer and Rowan's constructs of organizational structure and legitimacy, they observed that during the 1960s and 1970s, two-year institutions were garnering greater public support at the very time that their effectiveness in terms of student outcomes was declining.[3] Further, they suggested that widespread adoption of a comprehensive mission is a textbook example of DiMaggio and Powell's isomorphic organizational tendencies. In their view, the "mental sets of organizational elites" play a prominent role in shaping organizational interests—a clear example of how beliefs and values operating in community colleges guide organizational behavior.[4]

DEFINING INSTITUTIONAL LOGICS

Friedland and Alford pioneered research into institutional logics through their examination of central values guiding Western society. They argued that Western institutions have "a central logic—a set of material practices and symbolic constructions—that constitute its organizing principles and are available to organizations and individuals to elaborate." In their view, Western society operates on a series of precepts including capitalism, the bureaucratic state, democracy, family, and religion. Each of these precepts or "institutions" has a logic that is "symbolically grounded, organizationally structured, and politically defended."[5] Thornton and Ocasio applied this concept to organizations and refined our understanding of institutional logics:

> Both material and symbolic—they provide the formal and informal rules of action, interaction, and interpretation that guide and constrain decision-makers in accomplishing the organization's tasks and in obtaining social status, credit, penalties, and rewards in the process. These rules constitute a set of assumptions and values about how to interpret organizational reality, what constitutes appropriate behavior, and how to succeed.[6]

Research building on Friedland and Alford's work has interpreted institutional logics as rules or norms that bridge the gap between organizations and broader societal expectations, belief systems that articulate values that in turn delineate organizational forms, practices, and priorities, and parameters for social actors that help determine legitimacy.[7]

Influence of Logics on Individual and Organizational Action

At this juncture the reader will undoubtedly be asking: What is the relationship of institutional logics to the completion agenda in community colleges? The easy answer is that logics enable leaders and staff to make sense out of forces in their environment by prescribing and proscribing actions. They dictate actions under the guise of a *dominant logic* that reinforce an established set of beliefs and practices. Dominant logics establish collective identities, create rules of the game for decision making, provide order and structure, and dictate the amount of attention an organization should devote to a particular issue or problem. Each of the mechanisms explored shortly helps to explain the mindset and behavior of community college practitioners applied to prevailing issues and challenges.

Collective Identity. Logics help define appropriate behavior and activity within an industry (that is, postsecondary education) and within organizations (individual colleges) in the industry, but it is the interplay between individuals' views and beliefs and those of the industry that validate what is proper.[8] The collective identities established by dominant institutional logics are "an important theoretical construct because they help to explain connections that create a sense of common purpose and unity within an industry."[9]

The collective "social identity" that logics create for individual actors shapes how they view their role in the organization.[10] They also define the industry and help those external to the industry understand it.[11] For example, community colleges are widely viewed as committed to open admissions, and this implies a certain approach to serving students that is understood within and beyond the industry of postsecondary education.

Rules Providing Order and Structure. Alliances and interests that affect the power structure within an organization are reinforced by practices, procedures, and norms that are defined by institutional logics. Logics also determine the roles of leaders and staff within an organization, which in turn align with practices and beliefs characteristic of the industry. For example, in higher education there are categories of individuals that work within institutions such as administrators and faculty. These categories can be broken down further, for instance, from academic affairs to student services, which carry with them expectations and roles that shape the mindset and beliefs of individuals who fill positions. Institutional logics shape how individuals relate to others by virtue of their position and broader values of the organization and the industry.[12]

Attention Devoted to Issues and Challenges. The extent to which an organizational issue or problem is given attention is an additional mechanism determined by logics.[13] Logics not only guide the actions of individuals, but they also determine "which issues, contingencies, or problems need to be considered as relevant in the interaction among actors."[14] An example will help to illuminate this point. In the historical context of the community college access mission, the emphasis of staff has been on growth through optimization of the number of students who enroll each term. As a result, significant attention is paid to marketing and outreach to potential students and simplification and acceleration of admissions processes. If the logic was to be focused on student success, an emphasis other than growth would in all probability be prevalent.

To summarize, institutional logics influence the actions of individuals and organizations within an industry. Logics frame the collective identity of leaders and staff and what constitutes appropriate behavior. Logics also determine the makeup of processes and practices and have an important influence on the classification of actors in the organization and the work they do. Finally, logics dictate the problems and issues that receive attention in an organization. The relationship between logics and the actions of individuals and organizations is a baseline for understanding the role competing logics (for example, access and completion) play in a rapidly changing industry such as community college education.

Competing Institutional Logics

Logics compete when simultaneously contradictory values, norms, and beliefs collide. In research applying competing institutional logics to community colleges, Gumport found that college presidents are guided by one of two value systems. The first is an industry-oriented logic that emphasizes the economic value of two-year institutions, and the second focuses on the college as an educational enterprise with broader social value. While not directly related to the completion agenda, these findings are important because they suggest that the local context for the community college looms large in driving college priorities and that college leaders need to satisfy multiple competing external constituencies.[15]

A case study of institutional logics in public higher education in Massachusetts found convergence among policymakers and board members "on particular lines of choice and thinking that lead to similar policy conclusions."[16] This research sheds light on how the views of policymakers in many states are converging around an institutional logic that emphasizes educational attainment and student success. This is not to suggest that policymakers' sole focus is student access, but rather that there is a growing consensus at the state and national levels about the need to improve student outcomes.

The contested ground between access and success logics appears to be more pronounced at the college level, where college faculty, staff, and leaders must contend with the shift in values and beliefs in the context of work roles. Thornton and Ocasio stress that there is not a causal relationship between competing logics and institutional change, but rather the competition between dominant and emergent beliefs and practices creates a threshold for change.[17] Researchers have argued it is difficult to define "the process by which assumptions that define institutional logics are contested and changed"[18] and that relatively little is known about the organizational response to multiple logics. Research does, however, point to the temporary nature of competition between logics as an important element of the process by which logics change.[19]

As noted previously, one of the ways that institutional logics guide individual action is through the establishment of a collective identity. Several studies have suggested that the emergence of a competing logic (success) begins to diminish the shared identity within an industry that had previously been stable as a result of a dominant logic (access). For example, in his study of the nonprofit housing sector, Mullins found that conflicting logics create "field fragmentation" and it is this deterioration of a common identity that provides the opportunity for new logics to emerge.[20]

Building on the idea of fragmentation, other studies have revealed that individual actors will actively exploit gaps between existing and emerging social identities to promote institutional change. The capacity for individuals to manipulate conflicting perspectives to push for change is made possible by the emergence of competing institutional logics that challenge the legitimacy of dominant beliefs and practices.[21] In this book, the emergence of the competing logic of student success creates an environment for individual and organizational actors to contest the access logic that has been predominant within community colleges for the past several decades.

Much of the literature about competing institutional logics underscores the central role of individual actors in resisting or promoting conflict. These actors can be powerful individuals who seek to maintain the status quo or insurgents who are taking advantage of inconsistencies among existing beliefs and practices. Suddaby and Greenwood note that individuals who pursue institutional change are generally more cognizant of organizational contradictions and are motivated to act on inconsistencies.[22]

CONCLUSION

In a 2010 article, Terry O'Banion, President Emeritus, League for Innovation in the Community College, noted that the emerging "completion agenda" signifies a "tectonic shift in the community college zeitgeist."[23] He argued that, while improving student success is an important endeavor, there should be more consideration given to the unintended consequences of this national push. On the surface, a shift in focus from student access to success may seem minor. However, the implications in terms of governmental expectations and subsidies, program offerings, staffing, the types of students admitted, and the kinds of interventions employed to help students could be profound.

Similarly, a recent report from the American Association of Community Colleges titled *Rebalancing the Mission: The Community College Completion Challenge* highlights the issues two-year colleges are encountering in this evolving context.[24] The tension between breadth of mission and quality of service notwithstanding, policymakers and community leaders value the versatility and efficiency of colleges in managing these divergent functions.

College leaders are understandably hesitant to walk away from aspects of their mission that have contributed to the support they enjoy. However, a commitment to student success will require investment in more robust student support. Tight revenue streams suggest internal reallocation will be the only way to create sustainable funding to meet this need. College presidents will need to make tough choices to strike a reasonable balance.

This chapter delineated the components of a framework to guide examination of the completion agenda in community colleges. Logics, which are closely held beliefs and practices within an organization and industry, serve as the basis for evolution of a dominant logic that guides collective behavior. Dominant logics are not stable and can be challenged. Competing logics disrupt incumbent beliefs and social identities through the actions of individuals or organizations seeking change. Table 2.1 draws on recent research from Thornton, Ocasio, and Lounsbury and illustrates the competing logics of access and success confronting community colleges.[25]

The dominant access logic reflects the long-held view of community colleges as institutions that maximize convenience and access to a broad range of program choices and offerings through open admissions. The shift of the community college toward an insurgent logic emphasizing successful student outcomes begins to raise questions about who our colleges serve, at what cost, and under what conditions. The lens changes to credential attainment, which will lead colleges to consider a markedly different "set of material practices"[26] and rethink their strategy and mission to maintain legitimacy.

Table 2.1. Competing Institutional Logics in Community Colleges

Characteristics	Access Logic	Success Logic
Sources of legitimacy	Number of students enrolled and breadth of programs	Number of students receiving credentials
Sources of authority	Board of trustees, presidents, and local stakeholders	Governors, legislators, and foundations
Sources of identity	Community college as center of open opportunity	Community college as a purveyor of credentials
Basis of norms	Increase enrollment and scope of programs	Increase the number of credentials awarded
Basis of attention	Entry at the start of each academic term/year	Retention/completion at the end of each term/year/program
Basis of strategy	Grow number of "customers" through marketing and recruitment	Grow through the retention of current "customers"
Informal control mechanisms	Local influence	State and national influence
Economic system	Welfare capitalism	Market capitalism

Source: Adapted from Patricia H. Thornton, William Ocasio, and Micheal Lounsbury, *The Institutional Logics Perspective: A New Approach to Culture, Structure, and Process* (Oxford, UK: Oxford University Press, 2012).

To be successful in advocacy for change, the institutional change proponents must leverage enabling conditions—environmental shocks and their own standing within the organization—to create a vision that will mobilize allies and resources to their cause. The shift toward a market logic on the societal level, which for the purposes of this book has manifested in consensus about labor market demand for higher levels of education, has been promoted aggressively by foundations and policymakers. As a result, the focus on education attainment (that is, the emergent institutional logic) is challenging the long-held emphasis on access (that is, the dominant institutional logic) in open admissions colleges. The outstanding question is how community colleges will respond to and mediate shifting logics.

NOTES

1. John W. Meyer and Brian Rowan, "Institutionalized Organizations: Formal Structure as Myth and Ceremony," *American Journal of Sociology* 83, no. 2 (1977): 340–63.

2. Paul J. DiMaggio and Walter W. Powell, "The Iron Cage Revisited: Institutional Isomorphism and Collective Rationality in Organizational Fields," *American Sociological Review* 48, no. 2 (1983): 147–60.

3. Steven Brint and Jerome Karabel, "Institutional Origins and Transformations: The Case of American Community Colleges," in *The New Institutionalism in Organizational Analysis*, ed. Walter W. Powell and Paul J. DiMaggio (Chicago: University of Chicago Press, 1991), 337–60; Meyer and Rowan, "Institutionalized Organizations"; DiMaggio and Powell, "The Iron Cage Revisited."

4. DiMaggio and Powell, "The Iron Cage Revisited," 350.

5. Roger Friedland and Robert R. Alford, "Bringing Society Back In: Symbols, Practices, and Institutional Contradictions," in *The New Institutionalism in Organizational Analysis*, ed. Walter W. Powell and Paul J. DiMaggio (Chicago: University of Chicago Press, 1991), 232–63.

6. Patricia H. Thornton and William Ocasio, "Institutional Logics and the Historical Contingency of Power in Organizations: Executive Succession in the Higher Education Publishing Industry, 1958–1990," *American Journal of Sociology* 105, no. 3 (1999): 801–43.

7. Friedland and Alford, "Bringing Society Back In"; Renate E. Meyer and Gerhard Hammerschmid, "Changing Institutional Logics and Executive Identities: A Managerial Challenge to Public Administration in Austria," *American Behavioral Scientist* 49, no. 7 (2006): 1000–14; Barbara Townley, "The Institutional Logic of Performance Appraisal," *Organization Studies* 18, no. 2 (997): 261–85; Clodia Vurro, M. Tina Dacin, and Francesco Perrini, "Institutional Antecedents of Partnering for Social Change: How Institutional Logics Shape Cross-Sector Social Partnerships," *Journal of Business Ethics* 94 (2010): 39–53.

8. Wendy L. Currie and Matthew W. Guah, "Conflicting Institutional Logics: A National Programme for IT in the Organisational Field of Healthcare," *Journal of Information Technology* 22 (2007): 235–47; W. Richard Scott, Martin Ruef, Peter J. Mendel, and Carol A. Caronna, *Institutional Change and Healthcare Organisations* (Chicago: University of Chicago Press, 2000).

9. Trish Reay and C. R. Hinings, "Managing the Rivalry of Competing Institutional Logics," *Organization Studies* 30, no. 6 (2009): 629–52.

10. Hayagreeva Rao, Philippe Monin, and Rodolphe Durand, "Institutional Change in Toque Ville: Nouvelle Cuisine as an Identity Movement in French Gastronomy," *American Journal of Sociology* 108, no. 4 (2003): 795–843, 797.

11. Irene M. Herremans, M. Sandy Herschovis, and Stephanie Bertels, "Leaders and Laggards: The Influence of Competing Logics on Corporate Environmental Action," *Journal of Business Ethics* 89 (2009): 449–72; Rao, Monin, and Durand, "Institutional Change in Toque Ville"; Reay and Hinings, "Managing the Rivalry of Competing Institutional Logics."

12. Patricia H. Thornton and William Ocasio, "Institutional Logics," in *The Sage Handbook of Organizational Institutionalism*, ed. Royston Greenwood, Christine Oliver, Roy Suddaby, and Kerstin Sahlin (Los Angeles: Sage Publications, 2008), 99–129; Currie and Guah, "Conflicting Institutional Logics"; Friedland and Alford, "Bringing Society Back In"; Meyer and Hammerschmid, "Changing Institutional Logics and Executive Identities."

13. Thornton and Ocasio, "Institutional Logics."

14. Vurro, Dacin, and Perrini, "Institutional Antecedents of Partnering for Social Change," 43.

15. Patricia J. Gumport, "The Demand-Response Scenario: Perspectives of Community College Presidents," *Annals of the American Academy of Political and Social Science* 586 (2003): 38–61.

16. Michael N. Bastedo, "Convergent Institutional Logics in Public Higher Education: State Policymaking and Governing Board Activism," *The Review of Higher Education* 32, no. 2 (2009): 209–34, 229.

17. Thornton and Ocasio, "Institutional Logics."

18. Roy Suddaby and Royston Greenwood, "Rhetorical Strategies of Legitimacy," *Administrative Science Quarterly* 50, no. 1 (2005): 35–67, 65.

19. Royston Greenwood, Amalia Magán Díaz, Stan Xiao Li, and José Céspedes Lorente, "The Multiplicity of Institutional Logics and the Heterogeneity of Organizational Responses," *Organization Science* 21, no. 2 (2010): 521–39.

20. David Mullins, "Competing Institutional Logics? Local Accountability and Scale and Efficiency in an Expanding Non-Profit Housing Sector," *Public Policy and Administration* 21, no. 3 (2006): 6–24, 21.

21. Greenwood et al., "The Multiplicity of Institutional Logics and The Heterogeneity of Organizational Responses"; Meyer and Hammerschmid, "Changing Institutional Logics and Executive Identities"; Mullins, "Competing Institutional Logics?"; Anne-Claire Pach and Filipe Santos, "When Worlds Collide: The Internal Dynamics of Organizational Responses to Conflicting Institutional Demands," *Academy of Management Review* 35, no. 3 (2010): 455–76.

22. Suddaby and Greenwood, "Rhetorical Strategies of Legitimacy."

23. Terry O'Banion, "To What End?" *Inside Higher Ed*, August 16, 2010.

24. Christopher M. Mullin, *Rebalancing the Mission: The Community College Completion Challenge* (Washington, DC: American Association of Community Colleges, 2010).

25. Patricia H. Thornton, William Ocasio, and Micheal Lounsbury, *The Institutional Logics Perspective: A New Approach to Culture, Structure, and Process* (Oxford, UK: Oxford University Press, 2012).

26. Friedland and Alford, "Bringing Society Back In," 248.

THREE

Presidential Perspectives
on the Completion Agenda

This chapter explores interrelated dilemmas community colleges face as they attempt to respond to the mounting pressure of the completion agenda. The tensions examined include the sustainability of open access, the breadth of program offerings under constrained funding, and the ongoing challenge of maintaining quality. While individual colleges may address these issues differently, there is agreement that these challenges affect all institutions.

This chapter draws on interviews conducted with community college presidents in a Midwest state that has been involved in numerous national completion initiatives. The perspective of community college presidents is particularly valuable given the leadership role they play on campus as well as their position at the fulcrum of external pressures, college culture, and organizational practice.[1]

It is also important to understand how presidents view the mission of their colleges in order to discern their capacity and willingness to serve as change agents who will guide their institutions in a new direction. Dialogue with presidents indicates they are grappling with interrelated aspects of the completion agenda, including the role of open access, the breadth of program offerings, the implications of funding constraints, and the challenge of instructional quality. These themes reinforce the notion that competing logics of student access and student success are operating on community college campuses.

The themes of access, programmatic breadth, funding constraints, and instruction have been the subject of continuous analysis by scholars and writers as community colleges entered the twenty-first-century. These themes also track closely to dilemmas Norton Grubb articulated in the forword of a recent book, *Gateway to Opportunity?: A History of the Community College in the United States.*[2] Grubb notes that community colleges are faced with four dilemmas: 1) the dilemma of college for all, 2) the dilemma of comprehensiveness, 3) the dilemma of resources, and 4) the dilemma of instruction.

Each of these illuminates a historic strength of community colleges, but also pervasive challenges for these institutions in the future. This chapter is organized around these interrelated dilemmas—all with a bearing on the completion agenda—from the perspective of seated presidents.

DILEMMA OF COLLEGE FOR ALL

The open-door mission of community colleges is based on a philosophy of "college for all," but lax admissions requirements and a corresponding influx of students needing academic remediation present a significant dilemma for community colleges. Grubb and Lazerson suggest that the "education gospel," which calls for higher educational attainment as a solution to a wide range of societal issues, creates a dilemma that is particularly acute for community colleges.[3] Because community colleges are more accessible and affordable than other segments of higher education, they are a logical entry point for many students.

The challenge, of course, is that an open-door admissions policy results in a significant portion of students enrolling who are first-generation students, with little or no knowledge of the college-going experience and expectations. Additionally, a large number of these students are academically unprepared for college-level work. What follows is what presidents have to say about the dilemma of college for all.

An Unshakable Commitment to the Open Door

Community colleges were founded on the notion of providing access to a wide range of students regardless of preparation. Presidents doggedly embraced this philosophy and frequently indicated that a fundamental part of the institutional mission is to improve students' lives by providing access to higher education for those who may not otherwise have it. Citing efforts of four-year colleges and universities to increase admissions selectivity of their institutions and climb the ladder of prestige rankings (for example, U.S. News and World Report), presidents collectively see their institutions serving as an agent for social equity and justice that other sectors of postsecondary education overlook. One president emphatically stated that the community college is a source of opportunity that cannot be found elsewhere: "There are millions of people that would not have had any education beyond high school if it weren't for community colleges. They would not go to the university. First of all, many of them would not even be accepted. Second of all, they wouldn't have succeeded if they had gotten in." Another president, in describing the attraction of community colleges, stated that accessibility was what was appealing to him and that "open admission means that low-income people could go [to college] . . . who otherwise would not be able to go."

By definition open admissions colleges will take students regardless of their academic skills and readiness for college coursework. In many cases, the only limitation colleges place on prospective students is that they have a high school diploma or take the General Educational Development (GED) test. It is not uncommon for community colleges to work with local adult education providers to see that students complete the GED and progress into college. The sentiment of helping all students is reflected in the following quote from the president of a mid-size college:

> We meet every person where they are because we know there is a range of cognitive abilities and life experiences. We meet them where they are and then take them with great support and challenge and boundary setting to a new level of cognitive and emotional competence. To give folks a career that reflects what America does best—moving folks to a higher academic skill set and to a higher level of standard of living and economic viability.

This quote is indicative of many similar comments about the deep commitment of community colleges to providing students a first, and for many the only, chance to improve their position in life through postsecondary education.

The Barrier of Academic Readiness

A fundamental dilemma for community colleges is that open-door access leads to a student population with a wide variety of skill sets and colleges need to provide adequate support for students to progress and realize the promise of a postsecondary credential. This is especially true for students who are not ready for college-level courses at entry. A significant number of college presidents, while supportive of the open door, lament the substantial percentage of students requiring remediation. National research suggests that 60 percent of incoming community college students require at least one developmental education course.[4] According to many presidents, the problem is getting worse. The frustration generated is apparent in the following comment from a rural college president:

> More of our students are coming in developmentally challenged. Developmental education is very expensive to deliver. We're finding ourselves doing more and more of that. It is kind of a double whammy with funding cuts overall, then just having to put more resources into the developmental education. For example, our data from last fall show that 70 percent of our students tested into developmental education. This fall that went up to 79 percent! In one year, it increased nine percent.

The scope of the remediation problem at community colleges is worsening in some states as legislators and governors move to eliminate developmental education at four-year public universities. Citing the cost differential between community colleges and universities in the delivery of remediation, policymakers in some states are pushing for all developmental courses to be offered at two-year institutions. This has led some presidents to establish contracts for delivery of remediation with regional universities, while others express concern about the remedial component of the college mission and the possibility that it might overwhelm other functions.

Generally, presidents see remediation as a core component of the community college mission and a natural outgrowth of the open-access role their institutions perform, but there is clear frustration with the readiness of students entering community colleges—particularly those directly from high school. None of the presidents explicitly blame their local high schools for the high number of graduates that come to college unprepared, but a statement from a president of a suburban college sums up the sentiment:

> We're getting students from our high schools, which are considered to be pretty good high schools, that are coming in and testing in the 40 to 60 percent range [on the placement tests]—right at the developmental education level of either math or English. That's a sad statement there.

In spite of their frustration, many presidents cited greater collaboration with K–12 partners as an important part of improving college preparedness. In the end, however, community colleges can only do so much about this seemingly intractable problem. One rural college president bemoaned that "I can have a perfect machine of education and still the output may not be exactly what I'd like it to be based on the missing ingredient in that formula, which is the student's preparation and readiness."

Focus on College for All Unlikely to Diminish

Despite the challenges posed by the lack of college readiness, there is little doubt that the mantra of "college for all" will continue. State and federal policies for enhancing access, most notably the proposal for "free" community college by President Obama, have emerged as part of the completion agenda. These policies center on increasing the number of students in the postsecondary pipeline and are an important subtext to larger completion goals.

Record enrollment growth during the Great Recession led many to believe that growing enrollment to reach state goals would be easily achieved. This did not happen, however, as economic growth following the recession-flattened enrollments. Over the long term, this condition may serve as an impetus for more colleges to focus on student success, but elevating the number of students completing a credential is a significant challenge. The push for clear, data-driven attainment goals led one rural community college president to express the following concern about the open-door mission:

> I see a big shift and what I'm afraid of is that we'll start becoming primarily numbers driven. The students may wind up being the ones who lose in the long run, especially the ones that need a lot of help. Because the focus will be on retention and completion, the ones that are not strong enough or capable enough could very well fall by the wayside. We could put all our emphasis on resources and efforts on the ones that are going to complete so we can maximize our state funding. That scares me. Granted, states are up against it and they have their budget challenges that they have to face. I hope this door never closes. I've said this to my staff, I'm afraid that the door, open door, is starting to close.

This statement encapsulates the dilemma community colleges face with the college-for-all mindset counterbalanced by external pressure toward improved outcomes. The prevailing institutional logic favoring access over the past several decades has fostered accepting students wherever they are, regardless of their academic preparation. The emerging student success logic is challenging this mode of thought and raising the question of what access really means.

A president from a mid-size suburban college astutely pointed out that "we should be talking about creating access to change and creating opportunities as a result of the learning experience and learning environment and I think that creating access to failure is not doing the student any favors." This line of thinking represents a subtle but growing shift in emphasis that will challenge the long-held open-door mission of community colleges.

DILEMMA OF COMPREHENSIVENESS

Community colleges pride themselves on being responsive to the communities they serve. As they have grown in importance, they have been asked to take on more and more functions. While program and service growth adds to the legitimacy of institutions in the eyes of local residents, it raises a dilemma of comprehensiveness.[5] The ever-increasing demand on community colleges to become involved in a wider array of community activities raises a critical question about whether they are doing any of it well.

Community Responsiveness Drives College Offerings

Most of the presidents interviewed said they embrace the comprehensive mission of the community college that has evolved over the past several decades to include occupational and transfer offerings, remedial education, workforce and economic development, small business advising, and more. They cite college responsiveness to local communities as a key driver of program and service offerings. One president stated fervently, "If the college isn't serving its community, it's not doing its job."

Presidents' views on community responsiveness and programmatic comprehensiveness, similar to open-door access, reflect a deeply held value. They see their colleges as "community assets," which can "turn on a dime to meet local workforce needs." Many point out that their individual institution is distinct from other community colleges because of the unique needs of their local community. This leads to a different mix of offerings in terms of credit programs leading to a certificate or degree as well as noncredit programs geared toward short-term training. A president from a large college described it this way:

> You've got 1,200 of these colleges across the country enrolling 6.5 million students. The largest single sector of higher education in America, but every one of them is a little different because the communities they serve are different.

While there is no doubt that local communities have differing needs, the question remains whether the level of responsiveness presidents consistently espoused is sustainable.[6] None of the presidents suggested they were willing to withdraw from specific aspects of their mission, but one president stated pointedly that "we try to be too many things. We try to be all things to all people."

The tension about how much a community college can and should do in light of constrained resources and increasing numbers of students needing remediation is real and growing. Aside from expressing concern over budgetary cuts, none of the presidents identified mission functions that they could conceivably sacrifice to save money. One president from a rural college adamantly rejected the notion of scaling back the college mission:

> So are we going to say no to transfer students? No, we're not going to do job training. We can't do that! I mean America needs us. I'm a believer that we need to keep our traditional community college mission and resist the idea— when people say they've closed their doors, I want to just—before you close your doors to students, the president should take a pay cut.

Sustaining comprehensive quality programming will require more resources than can be derived from cutting presidential salaries, but the sentiment stubbornly expressed by this president is reflective of the broad commitment presidents have toward the comprehensive mission.

Breadth of Program Offerings Requires Balance

College presidents were generally supportive of a broad range of program offerings, but their perspective was shaped by the historical evolution of the college they were leading. Depending on their college's history and whether it emerged from a junior college transfer model or from a technical/occupational track, the presidents placed a differential emphasis on mission. For example, the president of a large metropolitan college that has historically been a transfer-oriented community college indicated that the transfer mission has "probably become more prominent and it's as much a pull now for the university as it is a push for community colleges." This was not a view shared by most presidents. Certainly, most presidents value transfer programs, but not at the expense of occupational/technical programs.

Beyond the boundaries of functions central to the community college mission are pursuits that are tangential to mission. One president was very concerned about the drive toward prestige: "Everybody's a wannabe. If you're a college, you wannabe a university . . . if you're a two-year college, my experience has shown you wannabe a four-year college . . . if you're a technical college, you wannabe a community college." The sentiment expressed by this president, while a minority view among those interviewed, is supported by the competition for rankings among universities[7] or the motivation of community colleges to gain the authority to offer bachelor's degrees.[8]

Their concerns about mission creep notwithstanding, presidents were generally interested in finding a balance between "dual role" occupational and transfer programming. One president argued that the dual role is critical because "for one student, you serve their purpose at the moment [with a technical program], but you don't close doors of opportunity for that student [to transfer and earn a bachelor's degree]." This same president suggested that, in the recent past, there was more of a focus on the transfer mission than technical programming, but the pendulum has started to swing in the other direction. He argued that external needs change and periodic shifts in emphasis are why dual roles at community colleges are important.

Another president echoed this point, but also suggested that it is the unique needs of students that contribute to the need for comprehensive programming:

Part of our goal is to fill gaps . . . if other institutions in the community are the bricks; in some ways we're the mortar. You know we're a bridge for all of our students to something else. Not necessarily a final destination. Students are coming here for a couple of classes or a short-term certificate or an Associate's degree to prepare them for a specific career or a specific job. Our students are coming here on their way to transfer to a Bachelor's degree. Our students are coming back here after starting at a university and kind of regrouping and then on their way back. So I think we meet a lot of unique needs for students who are in unique situations.

A number of presidents advocated for tighter integration of occupational and transfer programs to benefit both students and the institution. The president of a mid-size college suggested that community colleges should eliminate the distinction between occupational and transfer programs: "I think applied [training] gets you ready for a specific expertise. Liberal arts prepare you to do everything." This sentiment is indicative of a national trend that is just beginning to manifest itself. Practitioners and policymakers are calling for greater sophistication in the alignment between occupational programming—including short-term training—and degrees that are oriented toward the traditional transfer mission.

Global Economic Pressures Will Continue to Drive
Comprehensive Programming

Nearly all of the presidents interviewed indicated that the changing global economy and its impact on local communities will require that colleges serve a diverse population with an equally varied set of program offerings. Community colleges have become an important player in economic and workforce development,[9] and as the statement below suggests, this emphasis is not likely to subside.

We are in a place where the birth and death of industries and companies and jobs is on an accelerated scale. What does that require from an employee perspective or from a workforce perspective? It requires a lot more education, a lot more training, and a lot more retraining. It's a continuous education process. We've got a rapidly changing economy requiring new skills, new abilities, new knowledge, and new content, and you have a more rapid churning of employment causing people to have to stay in the educational process. So you've got huge change taking place.

Most presidents believe that their institutions are prepared to meet these demands, but some express caution about being overly responsive to the needs of communities. They point to concerns about balancing immediate needs of the local community with a long-term vision of what programmatic offerings can and should be. For example, colleges need to provide support for liberal arts programs that are relevant for students planning to transfer to a university in contrast to short-term occupational programming leading to a career. This may contradict what employers want. The following statement from the president of a large college captures this sentiment:

> I think it's really positive that community colleges have been tasked by society to be relevant. I think it's very positive that they prove their relevancy and their utility. I don't necessarily believe that all colleges and universities need to prove their relevance to the community. . . . I don't know that all research universities have to prove they are relevant on a day-to-day basis, but I do believe that community colleges should prove their relevance daily. I think on the flipside, and it is a double edged sword, we don't want to get too shortsighted and just get to the point of, well, "what did you do for us this week?" that was relevant.

This section has focused on programs offered by colleges in response to community needs and how balance is achieved between quality and breadth of offerings. A number of presidents take a broad view of mission and assert that in many communities no other institution but the community college will provide the needed service. Further, a number of presidents argue that without community colleges many in their communities would not make the transition to new economic realities, with a resulting negative impact on quality of life. While this may be true, the question of breadth and quality of programming represents a key dilemma for community colleges moving forward.

The access logic suggests that colleges should continue to provide a wide array of programs to support learners and communities; however, the success logic may challenge this assumption as institutions adjust to focus on helping students meet educational goals.

DILEMMA OF RESOURCES

A longstanding bragging point for community colleges beyond open admissions and comprehensive programming has been their affordability and operational efficiency relative to public four-year counterparts. As a lower-cost choice with open admissions, community colleges are an appealing option for low-income students. However, declining resources in most states and corresponding cuts in state subsidies for higher education are problematic for community colleges because the kinds of students they serve require significant supports to be successful.[10] Further, accountability for student outcomes and transparency of results is on the rise and community colleges are being asked to do more with less.

Colleges Embrace a Low-Cost Approach to Maximize Access

Community college tuition is a fraction of that at public universities. More specifically, according to the College Board, for the 2014–15 academic year, in-district tuition for full-time students at community colleges averaged $3,347. This stands in stark contrast to average in-state tuition at public four-year universities ($9,139) or the tuition average at private nonprofit universities ($31,231).

Presidents view the lower cost offered by community colleges as a critical aspect of the access mission. Asked about key elements of the mission of his college, a rural community college president indicated, "It is affordability." He further cited the strong commitment from the board of trustees to keep the college as an affordable option and stated: "We have the lowest tuition of any community college in the state. We are true to our mission."

Tuition in all sectors of higher education continues to increase, but presidents see the role of community colleges as a lower-cost option as critical to providing equitable postsecondary education opportunities for underrepresented and low-income groups. They also see the price differential as an important competitive advantage over other sectors of higher education. The following quote from the president of another rural college reflects this sentiment:

> Some universities are pricing themselves out of the marketplace, where at least we are helping them [students] get the first two years at $3,600 versus $36,000. That is one of my kind of stump speeches at the community meetings, to say "$3,600 gets you your first two years here and then you can go onto to X University or Y State University or wherever." So we provide a quality education close to home for a fraction of the price. It is an important piece of being "democracies colleges."

Low-cost has not only resulted in a competitive advantage for community colleges, it has also created goodwill among policymakers toward these institutions. One president described the perception legislators have of community colleges "as fairly accountable, efficient operations. I think there's opportunity for recognition of that sort of adding to the value proposition." While this supports the notion of advocacy from policymakers, this sentiment is counterbalanced by legislative initiatives such as adoption of outcomes-based funding, which have had a pervasive impact on resource flows to community colleges in the state.

Historically, higher education funding in most states has focused exclusively on enrollment—what can be labeled an access-based approach. Under this approach, colleges have been incentivized to focus on how many students enroll at the start of a semester. Clearly the emphasis on low tuition and full support by states over time contributed to a substantial increase in the number of students attending two-year institutions. One president from a mid-size institution characterized the situation in the past by stating, "If you weren't growing by ten percent, you were not meeting the need of the state."

However, in recent years there has been a shift in funding for community colleges based on student progression toward and successful completion of a credential. According to the website of the National Conference of State Legislatures, thirty-seven states have recently adopted or are in the process of adopting performance funding.[11] With this trend nationally, many of the presidents interviewed were resigned to the realities of outcomes-based funding, but some are pointedly skeptical, as the following quote illustrates:

> I think there's almost a naivety among those who sort of profess these things in the sense that they believe that by dangling some carrots we can actually change the conditions of learning, and we can actually get people to learn more rapidly, or to learn on our terms versus their terms. It's a complex thing that I haven't really got my arms around. I guess after all these years I really believe that people are going to learn when they want to learn. All the cajoling and the dangling of carrots won't make that much of a difference.

The implications of outcomes-based funding mechanisms are yet to be fully understood, but emerging research suggests that performance funding may not have as large an impact as its proponents would like to see. Research notwithstanding, it is clear that state policymakers have a different level of expectation for community colleges than they have exercised in the past and colleges are going to have to operate under new rules.

Accountability May Shift the Definition of Effectiveness and Efficiency

The heart of the resource dilemma for community colleges is the squeeze imposed by flat or declining state subsidies and simultaneous pressure to keep tuition low and improve student outcomes. In the words of a president:

> Accountability is at the center of the table right now and for mostly external reasons. The people that provide the money, they want to know their return on investment, and not only that, it has become evident to everybody, at least it should be evident today, that we brag about our successes and we ignore our failures and our failures are legion.

This statement highlights why the shift toward completion and student outcomes in state and federal accountability mechanisms is such a challenge for community colleges. The historic focus on enrollment and access played to the strength of these institutions, but the emphasis on what happens to students once they enroll forces colleges to address fundamental issues that challenge the notion of efficiency.

A president from a suburban college points out that historically colleges would "talk about how our populations were different, but this would often come across as us being defensive." He went on to say that as a sector, two-year institutions should stop "trying to explain away our failures rather than talking about what success looks like, how to determine that, and its difference for a community college." He suggested that community colleges should embrace how their student population is different and "their [students] reasons for coming here are different and obviously their outcomes are different." This approach may be reasonable and necessary moving forward, but it will raise uncomfortable questions that some presidents are ready to embrace and others are not.

One president welcomed the increased scrutiny, stating that "we are being held accountable—accountable for our resources and accountable for the success of our students. I see that as a good thing." Another president who had a long career in K–12 education where he dealt with significant accountability requirements was less sympathetic to those that push back against the growing emphasis on results. He bluntly stated, "Welcome to the club!" Still others are uneasy about the apparent disconnect between the core mission of the college and the growing emphasis on efficiency by policymakers. One longstanding president voiced the following concern:

> I see pressures to run our colleges more as a business today and to me that has to do with institutional effectiveness. A lot of people define effectiveness based on return on investment and all sorts of things like that, which I don't want to make excuses [for], but to me the emphasis has shifted away from what we're doing for people to more of how are we running the college as a business.

This statement elevates the question of what is meant by efficiency and effectiveness, and it raises a key question about whether the focus on a low-cost enrollment growth model is sustainable in an era of outcomes-based funding and increased accountability.

There are at least two important factors that have allowed community colleges to keep their tuition lower. The first is that community colleges focus squarely on teaching without the obligation of research that is prevalent at universities. This enables community college faculty to carry much larger course loads than their peers at four-year institutions. A valuable byproduct of the teaching focus has been smaller class sizes. A second factor that has kept cost down at community colleges has been their reliance on part-time or adjunct faculty.[12]

The ratio of full- and part-time faculty and class size will be covered in detail later in the chapter, but the resource dilemma colleges face impacts both factors substantially and each raises important questions about how to best support students.

Pressure to Do More with Less Will Continue

While the economic conditions that plagued state budgets during the Great Recession have eased, the longer view of state finances suggests that appropriations for higher education in general and community colleges in particular will not markedly improve. In addition, the rising cost of higher education for students will place considerable pressure on colleges to cap tuition. These dynamics suggest that there will not be an influx of additional resources for community colleges moving forward.

The likelihood of continuing resource constraint coupled with the growing emphasis on outcomes points to tough choices for community colleges moving forward. A recent survey of state directors of community college systems suggests that the completion agenda is made considerably more difficult with flat or declining state support.[13] However, there are indications that college presidents are beginning to move away from an exclusive focus on enrollment.

For example, a recently appointed president from a large urban college indicated that he is moving the college in a different direction from his long-serving predecessor. "In the past they were really busy growing and that caused short-term thinking that we're now trying to break out of." The following comment by a long-serving president echoed the need to shift the focus, but also raised important challenges in doing so:

> For decades the prime indicator was enrollment. Now that's shifted over the last few years. Now it's completion. With completion being the prime indicator and the prime determinate of funding, it's gotten everyone's attention. That's where it should be. Granted the Gates Foundation, the Lumina Foundation and others, that's where the focus is and the issues attendant to successful learning and completion. That's gotten everybody's attention and you open the strategic plan for the state that has real accountability, but we're still not successful where the game is played and that's the classroom, the laboratory. Part of it is faculty resistance. Part of it is institutional ignorance and institutional will.

Constrained resources will force colleges to make unpalatable operational decisions, for example, increasing historically small class sizes and growing the number of part-time faculty to accommodate budget challenges. These operational trends, which will be discussed in more detail in the next section, will maximize the fiscal circumstances of a college under an access-oriented institutional logic. However, these trends will run counter to the direction colleges need to pursue under a logic of student success and improved outcomes.

DILEMMA OF INSTRUCTION

Community college advocates often cite accessibility, affordability, and comprehensive program offerings as a central argument for the value of public two-year institutions. Another attribute frequently cited is the emphasis on teaching. Community college faculty are free from research and publishing obligations that are required of their university peers and therefore can focus more intensely on classroom instruction. While on the surface this is seemingly an advantage for community colleges, Grubb suggests that dynamics such as declining resources, increased needs for remediation among students, and a general lack of attention to quality teaching create a fourth and final dilemma—the dilemma of instruction.[14]

Teaching Institutions: An Important, but Uncertain, Moniker

Community colleges are often referred to as "teaching" or "student-centered" institutions. This distinction is made in the context of what community college instructors do compared to peers in other sectors of higher education. For example, community colleges have smaller class sizes, particularly when compared to large lecture prerequisite courses at universities for first-year students. Further, community college instructors focus squarely on teaching without the publishing and research expectations of professors at four-year institutions. This singular focus on teaching enables instructors to teach more classes per term—an important contributor to the operational efficiency of two-year institutions.[15]

In *Honored but Invisible: An Inside Look at Teaching in Community Colleges*, Grubb and his co-authors point out that simply because community colleges have smaller classes and instructors are not distracted by research requirements do not necessarily make these colleges "teaching institutions." In fact, community college leaders generally pay scant attention to the quality of instruction in the classroom. Leaders often rely on external perceptions of what their colleges are doing and, in reality, are no more focused on quality instruction than their peers at universities.[16]

Reinforcing this critique are college presidents who speak in general terms about teaching and learning at their institutions. In the Midwest they point to the role of a regional accreditor—the Higher Learning Commission (HLC) of the North Central Association of Colleges and Schools—as validation of the quality of instruction. Specifically, a number of presidents refer to college participation in the Academic Quality Improvement Program (AQIP). AQIP was launched by HLC in 1999 in an effort to establish ongoing dialogue with colleges and universities about continuous program improvement and to replace the ten-year visitation cycle of traditional accreditation.[17]

In comments about student achievement and program quality, one president indicated that as part of AQIP his college "has made steady progress toward enhancing student achievement through instructional improvement, tracking, focusing, and altering the iterative process; we've done a good job with that." When asked about their institutional and program effectiveness, several presidents cited the accreditation process as a gauge of how instructors think about their own performance. One commented:

> You also have to look at your faculty and staff in terms of how do they define performance? What is important to them? We look at things like accreditation. Accreditation is an important measure of how well we are performing and it isn't just the Higher Learning Commission, but it's all of the specialized professional accreditations that are out there. And I'm a believer in having every program that's eligible for one [accreditation] to have one because it is a way to get an independent outside investigation of your performance. You can have somebody else who's in the business come in and look at what you're doing and say yes you are measuring up. And I think that's an important part.

This statement is representative of the view of many of the presidents interviewed and likely of higher education leaders throughout the nation. However, the accreditation process has come under attack in recent years for a lack transparency and capacity to drive reform. Criticism of the accreditation process stems in part from a lack of institutional accountability for specific student learning outcomes.

Many of the presidents characterized the effectiveness of their institutions through the lens of helping students reach educational goals and objectives. However, as one president noted, "The question is, not only are students getting through, but what are they learning? I think we have a major crisis in this country when it comes to [learning] outcomes." Lingering concerns about the rigor of accreditation and learning outcomes assessments have been prevalent for some time, but the dilemma of instruction that community colleges face is exacerbated by operational impacts resulting from constrained resources and increased pressure for completion.

Limited Resources Put Considerable Strain
on Instructional Effectiveness

Despite rhetoric that practitioners use suggesting that community colleges are student-centered and focused on learning, operational decisions have been made that are detrimental to learning and outcomes. To counteract continuing reduction in state support, community colleges have moved to increase traditionally small class sizes. One president was surprisingly blunt about this strategy:

> We struggle to make the class sizes small. Yet, as we look into the future, those class sizes are going to have to become much larger just to make them economically viable. That may not be what a high school student would find in their best interest—a small class to us is currently 24, but it's going to become 36 and 48 as we move ahead.

Offering small classes and personal attention to students has been a hallmark of community colleges, but as one long-serving president indicated, "We don't have the luxury of small classes anymore."

While the size of classes is an important issue, the rise in the percentage of classes taught by adjunct faculty is a significantly more vexing problem and a growing challenge for community colleges. The percentage of courses taught by part-time, nontenured faculty is growing nationally.[18] In a recent article in the *Trusteeship Magazine* about the changing nature of the academic workforce, Kezar and Maxey noted that percentage of faculty that were adjunct or contingent had reached a level of 67 percent in 2009 compared with 22 percent in 1969. Community colleges account for the largest percentage of part-time faculty at 69 percent.[19]

The trend toward a greater proportion of courses with adjunct instructors is clearly increasing—a development that is cause for concern among a growing number of presidents:

> It's not uncommon to find more than 50 percent of the faculty as part timers. Now, we've spun this yarn forever. "Oh, but those part-time faculty members, they're experts in their field. They really lend credibility to our institution. They really know what they're teaching." From a practical point of view, do they teach the critical thinking skills that are necessary for students to be able to elevate the kind of learning that goes on in the classroom?

This quote raises important questions about the quality of instruction provided by part-time faculty. Several researchers have examined the effect of part-time instruction on student success, and their findings have been largely negative. This is not surprising given the fact that many part-time faculty are detached from campus, receive very little professional development or support, and have limited interaction with students outside the classroom.[20]

Couple the dynamics of increasing numbers of adjunct faculty with a growing population of academically underprepared students and the situation goes from bad to worse. One president, who was generally pessimistic about the prospects created by this circumstance, suggests that "we're a miserable failure. Part of that, and I can only speak for community colleges, is that we have too many part-time instructors." Placing the dilemma of instruction in context with the shift from an institutional logic of student access to one that emphasizes success can only lead to the conclusion that community college instructional delivery models will change dramatically in the future.

INTERCONNECTED DILEMMAS

Recapping the four dilemmas discussed in this chapter—college for all, comprehensiveness, resources, and instruction—it is easy to identify the strategic choices that colleges could make to mitigate the challenges embedded in each dilemma. Community colleges could institute an admission standard that would curtail the number of underprepared students requiring remediation. The upside of this choice would be reallocation of scarce resources from developmental education to a wide array of programmatic offerings in support of student and community needs. The downside would be abandonment of the open-door philosophy that has distinguished community colleges since their founding.

Another choice colleges could make would be to eliminate programs that are expensive, for example, occupational programs that require costly equipment. The resources from discontinued programs could be used to hire additional full-time instructors and to support professional development opportunities for instructors. Again, this choice would force colleges to abandon programs that have been deemed important by the communities they serve—a circumstance almost certain to have an adverse effect.

These are but two examples of strategic choices available to community colleges to address the dilemmas they face. Our colleges, however, have core purposes that place boundaries on decision making. For example, the notion of *college for all* is a universal element in mission statements and is captured through such words as "educational opportunity," "access," and "life-long learning."

Similarly, the concept of *comprehensiveness* is described in most, if not all, college statements through a list of extensive program offerings or terms like "community resources" and "responsive." "Affordability" is both explicit and implied in statements of access embedded in mission statements. In all instances, the concept of *resources* is indirectly addressed through college statements as well. Finally, colleges address *instruction* in their mission statement by referring to constructs such as "quality education" and "student-centered learning."

This chapter has examined presidents' views through the lens of the dilemmas colleges face in regard to mission, effectiveness, and expectations. The perspectives represented herein are reflective of presidents' personal opinions. Because of the position they hold in the administrative hierarchy, their views also represent the direction and values of the entire organization. The dilemmas described in this chapter are real and they are becoming more acute as the student success logic gains momentum.

NOTES

1. Marilyn Amey, "Leadership as Learning: Conceptualizing the Process," *Community College Journal of Research and Practice* 29 (2005): 689–704; George R. Boggs, "Leadership Context for the Twenty-First Century," *New Directions for Community Colleges* 123 (2003): 15–25; Paul L. Dressel, "Mission, Organization, and Leadership," *The Journal of Higher Education* 58, no. 1 (1987): 101–9; John S. Levin, "Presidential Influence, Leadership Succession, and Multiple Interpretations of Organizational Change," *The Review of Higher Education* 21, no. 4 (1998): 405–25; Christopher W. Shults, *The Impact of Presidential Behaviors on Institutional Movement towards Greater Abundance in Community Colleges: An Exploratory Study* (Ann Arbor, MI: University of Michigan, 2009); George B. Vaughan and Iris M. Weisman, *The Community College Presidency at the Millennium* (Washington, DC: American Association of Community Colleges, 1998).

2. Josh M. Beach, *Gateway to Opportunity?: A History of the Community College in the United States* (Sterling, VA: Stylus Publishing, 2011).

3. W. Norton Grubb and Marvin Lazerson, *The Education Gospel: The Economic Power of Schooling* (Cambridge, MA: Harvard University Press, 2004).

4. Thomas Bailey, Dong Wook Jeong, and Sung-Woo Cho, "Referral, Enrollment, and Completion in Developmental Education Sequences in Community Colleges," *Economics of Education Review* 29, no. 2 (2010): 255–70; Catherine Horn, Zoë McCoy, Lea Campbell, and Cheryl Brock, "Remedial Testing and Placement in Community Colleges," *Community College Journal of Research and Practice* 33, no. 6 (2009): 510–26; Katherine L. Hughes and Judith Scott-Clayton, "Assessing Developmental Assessment in Community Colleges," *Community College Review* 39, no. 4 (2011): 327–51.

5. Beach, *Gateway to Opportunity?*

6. David Ayers, "Community Colleges and the Politics of Sociospatial Scale," *Higher Education* 62, no. 3 (2011): 303–14; George R. Boggs, "Community Colleges in the Spotlight and Under the Microscope," *New Directions for Community Colleges* 156 (2011): 3–22; Debra D. Bragg, "Community College Access, Mission, and Outcomes: Considering Intriguing Intersections and Challenges," *Peabody Journal of Education* 76, no. 1 (2001): 93–116; Sean Ajay Desai, "Is Comprehensiveness Taking Its Toll on Community Colleges? An In-Depth Analysis of Community Colleges' Missions and Their Effectiveness," *Community College Journal of Research and Practice* 36, no. 2 (2012): 111–21; Kevin J. Dougherty, "The Evolving Role of the Community College: Policy Issues and Research

Questions," *Higher Education: Handbook of Theory and Research* 17 (2012): 295–348; Duane E. Leigh and Andrew M. Gill, "How Well Do Community Colleges Respond to the Occupational Training Needs of Local Communities? Evidence from California," *New Directions for Community Colleges* 146 (2009): 95–102; Christopher M. Mullin, *Rebalancing the Mission: The Community College Completion Challenge* (Washington, DC: American Association of Community Colleges, 2010).

7. Michael N. Bastedo and Nicholas Bowman, "College Rankings as an Interorganizational Dependency: Establishing the Foundation for Strategic and Institutional Accounts," *Research in Higher Education* 52 (2011): 3–23; Marc Meredith, "Why Do Universities Compete in the Rankings Game? An Empirical Analysis of the Effects of the U.S. News and World Report College Rankings," *Research in Higher Education* 45 (2004): 443–61; James Monks and Ronald G. Ehrenberg, *The Impact of U.S. News and World Report College Rankings on Admissions Outcomes and Pricing Policies at Selective Private Institutions* (Cambridge, MA: National Bureau of Economic Research, 2004).

8. John S. Levin, "The Community College as a Baccalaureate-Granting Institution," *The Review of Higher Education* 28, no. 1 (2004): 1–22; Barbara K. Townsend, "A Cautionary View," in *The Community College Baccalaureate: Emerging Trends and Policy Issues*, ed. Deborah L. Floyd, Michael L. Skolnik, and Kenneth P. Walker (Sterling, VA: Stylus Publishing, LLC., 2005), 1–7.

9. Richard L. Alfred, "The Future: Mastering the Contradiction," *Community College Journal* 72, no. 3 (2002): 10–14; Ayers, "Community Colleges and the Politics of Sociospatial Scale"; Boggs, "Community Colleges in the Spotlight and Under the Microscope"; Jason Lee Davis, "Community Colleges: The Preferred Provider of Career and Technology Education and Training," *Community College Journal of Research and Practice* 32, no. 8 (2008): 568–72; John A. Downey, Brian Pusser, and J. Kirsten Turner, "Competing Missions: Balancing Entrepreneurialism with Community Responsiveness in Community College Continuing Education Divisions," *New Directions for Community Colleges* 136 (2006): 75–82; James Jacobs and Kevin J. Dougherty, "The Uncertain Future of the Community College Workforce Development Mission," *New Directions for Community Colleges* 136 (2006): 53–62; Michelle Van Noy and James Jacobs, "The Outlook for Noncredit Workforce Education," *New Directions for Community Colleges* Summer (2009): 87–94.

10. Beach, *Gateway to Opportunity?*

11. "Performance-Based Funding for Higher Education," *National Conference of State Legislatures*, last modified July 31, 2015, http://www.ncsl.org/research/education/performance-funding.aspx.

12. Hara D. Charlier and Mitchell R. Williams, "The Reliance On and Demand for Adjunct Faculty Members in America's Rural, Suburban, and Urban Community Colleges," *Community College Review* 39, no. 2 (2011): 160–80; Chad Christensen, "The Employment of Part-Time Faculty at Community Colleges," *New Directions for Higher Education* 143 (2008): 29–36; John S. Levin, "Multiple Judgments: Institutional Context and Part-Time Faculty," *New Directions for Community Colleges* 140 (2007): 15–20.

13. Stephen G. Katsinas, Mark M. D'Amico, and Janice Nahra Friedel, *Challenging Success: Can College Degree Completion Be Increased as States Cut Budgets?* (Tuscaloosa, AL: University of Alabama, Education Policy Center, 2011).

14. Beach, *Gateway to Opportunity?*

15. Arthur M. Cohen and Florence B. Brawer, *The American Community College*, fifth edition (San Francisco: Jossey-Bass Publishers, 2008); W. Norton Grubb, Helena Worthen, Barbara Byrd, Elnora Webb, Norena Badway, Chester Case, Stanford Goto, and Jennifer Curry Villeneuve, *Honored but Invisible: An Inside Look at Teaching in Community Colleges* (New York: Routledge, 1999); Barbara K. Townsend, "Community College Faculty: Overlooked and Undervalued," *ASHE Higher Education Report* 32 (2007): 1–163.

16. Grubb et al., *Honored but Invisible*.

17. North Central Association, Higher Learning Commission, *Academic Quality Improvement Program: Introduction to AQIP* (Chicago, IL: The Higher Learning Commission, 2007).

18. Charlier and Williams, "The Reliance On and Demand for Adjunct Faculty Members in America's Rural, Suburban, and Urban Community Colleges"; Kevin Eagan, "A National Picture of Part-Time Community College Faculty: Changing Trends in Demographics and Employment Characteristics," *New Directions for Community Colleges* 140 (2005): 5–14; Susan Twombly and Barbara K. Townsend, "Community College Faculty: What We Know and Need to Know," *Community College Review* 36, no. 1 (2008): 5–24.

19. Adrianna Kezar and Daniel Maxey, "The Changing Academic Workforce," *Trusteeship Magazine*, May/June 2013.

20. Charlier and Williams, "The Reliance On and Demand for Adjunct Faculty Members in America's Rural, Suburban, and Urban Community Colleges"; Christensen, "The Employment of Part-Time Faculty at Community Colleges"; Eagan, "A National Picture of Part-Time Community College Faculty"; Donald W. Green, "Adjunct Faculty and the Continuing Quest for Quality," *New Directions for Community Colleges* 140 (2007): 29–39; Daniel Jacoby, "Effects of Part-Time Faculty Employment on Community College Graduation Rates," *The Journal of Higher Education* 77, no. 6 (2006): 1081–103; Levin, "Multiple Judgments"; John P. Murray, "Faculty Development in Publicly Supported Two-Year Colleges," *Community College Journal of Research and Practice* 25, no. 7 (2001): 487–502; Desna L. Wallin, "Part-Time Faculty and Professional Development: Notes from the Field," *New Directions for Community Colleges* 140 (2007): 67–73.

FOUR

Emerging Consensus Embedded in Research, Policy, and Practice

While there is no "silver bullet" for dealing with the complex problems that contribute to low completion rates, there are key areas of agreement in the field that are beginning to emerge. This chapter provides an overview of the findings from the research literature, examines field practices that are showing promise, and explores the levers that policymakers are using to promote completion.

Fortunately, key findings from research are reinforcing the experience of institutions. Additionally, policymakers are working thoughtfully to create conditions for colleges to support implementation of practices that scholarly research suggests make a difference. This chapter explores how the interplay between research, practice, and policy is shaping the completion agenda.

SYNTHESIS OF COMMUNITY
COLLEGE COMPLETION RESEARCH

There has been a substantial amount of research over the past several decades directed to persistence, retention, and completion, but it wasn't until the past five to ten years that much of this work was focused specifically on community colleges. The findings in some of these studies are summarized shortly, but it is useful to first review what the literature has to say about educational attainment of community college students and, more specifically, the impact of developmental education.

Education Attainment of Students Attending Community Colleges

Much of the literature on educational attainment focuses on the impact community college attendance has on students aspiring toward a baccalaureate degree. None of this work is more prominent than that of Brint and Karabel. In their seminal work *The Diverted Dream*, they drew on the idea of "cooling out" first articulated by Clark in 1960 and argued that students attending community colleges are redirected in their educational aspiration toward technical occupations and away from the pursuit of a baccalaureate degree. Brint revisited this argument and suggested that the factors leading to their original conclusion had worsened as more students from lower socioeconomic classes enrolled in community colleges.[1]

In contrast, Rosenbaum, Deil-Amen, and Person, in a more recent study on the impact of community colleges on student educational attainment, take exception with studies keyed to the cooling out function. They argue that previous studies do not adequately consider student educational goals and assume that most aspire to a degree. Bahr's work on student behavior and the varied ways they use community colleges reinforces this point by indicating that there are—as community college advocates have long argued—a considerable number of "skill-building" students who enroll for a few classes to augment job skills. According to Bahr, this group of students is largely successful in the courses they take, but never intended to acquire a degree. Rosenbaum, Deil-Amen, and Person argue that traditional cooling out studies do not account for this phenomenon, but after correcting for this problem, find that community colleges actually increase student aspirations through a process called "warming up."[2]

While the work of Bahr, Rosenbaum, and others sheds light on important nuances about student intent and its relationship to outcomes, there is no question that the success rate of students who start at a community college with a goal of getting a bachelor's degree is not what one would expect. As a result, questions about the wisdom of students starting at community colleges continue. There is little doubt that community colleges expand access to postsecondary education, and a number of studies have confirmed that states with a more highly developed network of community colleges enjoy higher participation levels in college.

What has also been established through research is that students who begin their college experience at a community college are less likely to attain a bachelor's degree. Student intent and preparation are among the most cited obstacles. Researchers have controlled for these characteristics and still found that students starting at a community college were less likely to attain a bachelor's degree than those enrolling in four-year institutions. Long and Kurlaender's study found that even when controlling for student and institutional characteristics (for example, socioeconomic status and college size) that are frequently cited as reasons for noncompletion, community college students were 14.5 percent less likely to complete a bachelor's degree after nine years.[3]

Nagging questions remain about the impact of enrolling at a community college and its effect on baccalaureate degree attainment. A number of studies have also examined the success rate of community college students who transfer to universities. These studies examine the performance of native students, who initially enroll in a four-year college or university, compared to students that transfer from a community college. The results are mixed, but they do suggest that students who transition successfully from community colleges perform as well as those starting at four-year institutions.[4] Another bright spot in this research is the tendency of students initially enrolling in community colleges to perform better in terms of sub-baccalaureate completion rates than their counterparts entering four-year institutions.[5]

Why does attendance at community colleges hinder bachelor's degree attainment? Brint and Karabel argue that the expanding vocational emphasis of two-year institutions has diverted capable students to sub-baccalaureate technical programs. Roska asserts that the vocational focus is not the problem. The growing emphasis on short-term certificate programs could be a causative factor because these programs divert students from degree programs. This perspective is logical given that many community college students attend part time and work multiple jobs.[6]

In a 2014 study Monaghan and Attewell challenged previous research pointing to academic preparation of students transferring from community colleges as a factor underlying low baccalaureate completion rates. Instead they found that completion was influenced by the loss of credits as students made the transition between institutions. Fewer than 60 percent of students were able to transfer most of their credits and as many as 15 percent of transfer students were not able to transfer any credits at all. Overall, Monaghan and Attewell found the loss of credits after transfer to be the most significant obstacle to completion of a baccalaureate degree.[7]

Another factor related to low attainment rates for students attending community colleges is "social know-how."[8] Deil-Amen and Rosenbaum argue that the knowledge and skills needed to navigate life as a community college student are comparable to those required at a four-year institution, yet two-year institutions don't do enough to impart this knowledge to those who enroll. They highlight seven obstacles community college students face because they lack knowledge of the college-going experience via family or friends: 1) bureaucratic hurdles, 2) confusing program choices, 3) student-initiated guidance, 4) limited counselor availability, 5) poor advice from staff, 6) slow detection of costly mistakes, and 7) poor handling of conflicting demands. The construct of limited social know-how draws on research about transfer "shock" and the period of adjustment for students who transition from community colleges to four-year colleges and universities. These studies point to the importance of a receptive culture at receiving institutions for transfer students.[9]

In closing this discussion about the influence of community college attendance on attainment of bachelor's degrees, it is worthwhile to note recent studies that suggest that having an associate degree in hand before a student transfers may increase the likelihood that they will earn a baccalaureate degree. A descriptive analysis by the National Student Clearinghouse indicates that 16 percent more transfer students completed baccalaureate degrees if they had already earned an associate degree compared to those who transferred without earning a two-year credential.[10] Analyses examining the impact of associate degree completion on baccalaureate degree attainment in a state university system suggest that students are more likely to earn a four-year degree if they first complete a two-year degree.[11]

These studies suggest that practitioners need to think differently about the value of an associate degree in relationship to the baccalaureate. While more research is needed to understand this relationship, this recent research suggests that a positive relationship between two-year and four-year degree attainment may reflect the ease of transferring credits for students with an associate degree compared to students with credits that fall short of the degree. If this relationship holds up under further scrutiny, an argument could be made that more students on a transfer trajectory should acquire the associate degree first. This would also mean that community colleges need to step up to this challenge and put students in a position to do so.

Incidence of Developmental Education and Impact on Students

As noted earlier, one of the major hurdles to degree completion for community college students is that many enroll needing academic remediation in one or more subjects. A significant amount of literature over the past decade has examined the efficacy of developmental education for students who are not college ready. Before turning to the effectiveness of developmental education, it is useful to examine the distribution of students in remedial courses. According to a recent study published by the Community College Research Center using national data, 68 percent of community college students and 40 percent of public four-year college students take at least one developmental education course. Only 28 percent of community college students who took a remedial course completed a degree within eight years. Further, many students placing into developmental education courses fail to complete the sequence of courses leading up to regular college courses.[12]

It is important to understand the background of students enrolling in developmental courses. According to this same CCRC report, 60 percent of all black students and 62 percent of all Hispanic students took a remedial course compared to 46 percent of white students. Further, 58 percent of students from families with incomes of less than $32,000 enrolled in a remedial course compared to 38 percent of those in the highest income bracket ($92,000 or more). These statistics illustrate racial and socioeconomic disparities among those enrolling in developmental education courses.[13]

Age differences are evident among students enrolling in developmental education courses. This distinction is important because colleges often conflate who actually needs remediation and why. For example, 46 percent of students eighteen years old or younger enrolled in a remedial course compared to 54 percent of individuals twenty-four years and older enrolling in college after being out for some time. Arguably a portion of this latter group needs a refresher because math or writing skills have not been used for some time. Not surprisingly, 57 percent of students who took a remedial course did not have a high school diploma or certificate and as a result carried weak basic skills to college.[14]

As these statistics illustrate, college leaders and staff should be careful not to treat students enrolled in remedial courses as a monolith. Students enter postsecondary education with a variety of needs and levels of preparation and one-size-fits-all solutions are unlikely to adequately address the issue of college readiness. That said, leaders and staff should not be complacent about the percentage of students requiring remedial courses—particularly students right out of high school—as their level of preparation is nowhere near where it needs to be in order to realize attainment goals.

A closer look at the efficacy of developmental education through the work of researchers suggests that the impact of remedial courses on student outcomes is negligible.[15] More specifically, in a recent overview of research CCRC examined seven rigorous studies of developmental education outcomes in six states using regression discontinuity—a methodology comparing outcomes using placement test scores for students above and below the "cut score" for remedial and college-level course placement. They found, with a couple exceptions, that developmental courses in math, reading, and writing had mostly no impact on student outcomes and in some instances actually had negative effects.[16]

These findings reinforce the notion that developmental education as delivered today is broken and in need of change. Further, they lend support to the idea that placing students who are close to college ready but just below the cut score into the gatekeeper (college-level) courses is empirically sound. Regression discontinuity studies have raised questions about the efficacy of assessment tests colleges use to gauge student readiness and procedures colleges use to place students in developmental or college-level courses.

According to research, the vast majority of community colleges use one of two tests to place students—ACCUPLACER developed by the College

Board or COMPASS developed by ACT whose use has recently been discontinued. Regardless of the assessment colleges use, test scores are not predictive of student outcomes, and many students end up underplaced in developmental education courses rather than college-level courses. Studies using high school grades, placement test scores, and demographic information to validate the accuracy of student placements suggest that of the 81 percent of students placed in remedial English, 29 percent were underplaced and could have been placed in a higher-level course. Similarly, of the three-quarters of students placed in developmental math, 18 percent should have been placed in a higher-level course. These studies raise critical questions about the reliance on assessments used to determine student academic readiness.[17]

The accuracy of placement tests takes on added importance when considering the impact of remedial course sequences on student progression into college-level courses. In a groundbreaking study by CCRC, researchers examined student progression through remedial course sequences and found that among 63,650 students at Achieving the Dream colleges placing into three remedial courses below college-level math, only 11 percent eventually passed the gatekeeper math course. Further, one out of four (26 percent) of the students never enrolled in the first course in the sequence. Of those that did enroll and made it through all three developmental math classes, 4 percent did not enroll in the college-level course. These data suggest that although a significant number of students successfully complete remedial courses, the overall course sequence may be too long for them and credit course enrollment is by no means a certainty. This research along with the regression discontinuity studies have spurred efforts toward acceleration through development course sequences as well as consideration of strategies to avoid remedial courses altogether.[18]

*Research on Institutional Characteristics and Practices
that Contribute to Completion*

Pressure from foundations and policymakers to improve completion rates has led to research about the institutional characteristics and practices that contribute to improved student outcomes. In an article about the challenges and opportunities community colleges face when attempting to increase completion rates, Goldrick-Rab argued that reform efforts must occur on multiple levels if student outcomes are to improve. She suggested three levels of reform: 1) a macro-level opportunity structure focused on issues of funding, governance, incentives, and other connected social policies that impact educational institution; 2) institutional or campus-level reforms that impact student outcomes such as access to credit-bearing coursework, pedagogical practices, the role of faculty, informational requirements, and organizational learning; and 3) individual student-level reforms aimed at social inequalities affecting success such as at-risk student characteristics, academic challenges, economic challenges, social and information hurdles, and attendance patterns.[19]

Goldrick-Rab's approach to reform is useful and parallels multilevel aspects of the competing institutional logics framework outlined in chapter 2. Reforms at the macro level and institutional level parallel the discussion in this chapter about state policy and institutional practices. Student considerations have been the focus of substantial research and are beyond the scope of this book. College-level reforms impacting student progression and completion are the heart of this chapter and the literature in this area is explored shortly.

Early studies of campus-level factors impacting student outcomes were conducted by CCRC in collaboration with the Achieving the Dream initiative.[20] In these studies, characteristics adversely impacting student success were identified, including a negative relationship between graduation rates and institutional size, the percentage of minority students enrolled, the percentage of students attending part time, and the number of adjunct faculty. These studies also found a positive relationship between spending on instruction and student services and graduation rates.

The negative relationships between institutional size and minority enrollment and success rates are not surprising given the propensity of greater numbers of academically underprepared minority students to enroll in large urban colleges. Sadly, this parallels conventional wisdom about achievement gaps among various student subgroups. On the positive side, however, is the favorable relationship between expenditures and outcomes suggesting that steps can be taken to improve student outcomes if leaders and institutions have the will to increase funding for success-focused initiatives.

CCRC published a series titled the Assessment of Evidence Series to document efforts within community colleges to improve student outcomes. After an exhaustive review of the literature describing promising practices and policies, a series of eight papers was published highlighting four steps institutions can take to improve the likelihood of student success:

1. Colleges should work to simplify the structures and bureaucracies that students must navigate.
2. Broad engagement of all faculty should become the foundation for policies and practices to increase student success. This should include active faculty involvement in student support activities.

3. Colleges should be encouraged to align course curricula, define common learning outcomes and assessments, and set high standards for those outcomes.
4. Colleges should collect and use data to inform a continuous improvement process.[21]

One of the most important findings advanced in the Assessment of Evidence Series was the observation that colleges are not student friendly. College policies and practices are often confusing and leave too much discretion to students who are not familiar with the college experience. An article describing promising practices in California community colleges suggests four criteria colleges need to adopt to better support students: more cohesion in programming, improved cooperation between college departments, improved connections with students, and greater consistency in college policy and practice. In the Assessment of Evidence papers, Karp builds on these points with the observation that programs resulting in positive student outcomes involve one or more of the following mechanisms: 1) creating social relationships, 2) clarifying aspirations and enhancing commitment, 3) developing college know-how, and 4) making college life feasible.[22]

In an article titled "The Pursuit of Student Success: The Directions and Challenges Facing Community Colleges," Hagedorn identified many of the same challenges articulated in chapter 3 that community colleges face in implementing strategies to improve student success. She outlined programs and interventions colleges are adopting, including student success courses, learning communities, structured mentoring, intrusive advising for academic and financial aid purposes, supplemental instruction, monitoring of mandatory placements, course-taking patterns, and concurrent enrollment with K–12 districts. In each instance she identified institutions working with innovative success practices, the impact evidenced for students, and prospects for scaling these practices to other student populations.[23]

The strategies Hagedorn described address many of the shortcomings in "social know-how" that Deil-Amen and Rosenbaum, Karp, and others have identified as obstacles to student success. Much of Deil-Amen and Rosenbaum's work on student engagement has its origins in the work of Tinto and his theory of student departure. Tinto has also weighed in on current research related to the completion agenda in *Completing College*. This follow up to his widely cited book *Leaving College* focuses on the need for colleges to rethink how they operate, specifically how colleges can do a better job helping students set expectations, providing enhanced support on a consistent basis, offering ongoing assessment and feedback, and enhancing the faculty role in improving student outcomes.[24]

Having highlighted some of the more prominent research of the past ten years, we now turn to a discussion of practices undertaken by colleges to improve student progression and success. In many if not most cases, these practices surfaced in response to research highlighting initiatives that work in student success.

CONVERGENCE AMONG INSTITUTIONAL PRACTICES

Areas of agreement about innovative strategies and interventions at individual colleges contributing to improved outcomes are increasingly evident. Examples of innovations include college commitment and focus on student success, greater use of data to improve programs and services, streamlined pathways to credentials and careers, and integrated student support services. Table 4.1, adapted from a report by the Institute of

Table 4.1. Institutional Practices Contributing to Student Success

Category	Examples of practices
College commitment and focus on student success	Strategic plan focused on student success; collaborative environment between academic and student affairs focused on student needs; leadership commitment to improving student outcomes
Use of data to improve programs and services	Using data to prioritize actions: institutional researchers track student outcomes; colleges collect data to inform a continuous improvement process
High-quality instruction with engagement from the faculty	Faculty have high expectations for students and help students see meaningful pathways to their goals; faculty development focused on improving teaching; accelerated or contextualized learning, particularly in developmental education; experiential learning
Streamlined pathways to credentials and careers	Clear college readiness standards; coherent programs of study with roadmap to completion of programs; career pathways with stackable credentials
Ongoing advising and monitoring student progression	Colleges provide sufficient resources for core advising function to ensure adequate ratios between advisors and students; colleges streamline bureaucratic processes; mandatory advising and orientation are in place
Integrated student supports and services	Student success or life skill courses are mandatory for students who are academic unprepared; learning communities or paired courses establish cohort learning; early warning and intrusive advising systems are in place to support at-risk students promptly

Source: Adapted from Institute of Higher Education and Policy. Caroline West, Nancy Syvlock, and Colleen Moore, *Measuring Institutional Conditions that Support Student Success in California Community Colleges* (Sacramento, CA: Institute of Higher Education and Policy, 2012).

Higher Education Leadership and Policy, provides an overview of specific practices advanced as part of the reform movement.[25] Some practices
have focused on improving student support or integrating services with
academic affairs through functions such as intrusive advising, learning
communities, supplemental instruction, and student success courses.
Other practices have focused on college-wide efforts to build commitment for student success through strategic planning and greater use of
data to inform decision making.[26]

A significant amount of work has been carried out over the past decade
to tackle issues that inhibit student success and completion. It is impos-
sible to capture all of this activity in one volume. The discussion that
follows is intended to highlight examples from the field drawn primarily
from national initiatives. This discussion is not intended as an exhaustive
survey of the activity that has been carried out on a national scale. The
categories of institutional practices outlined in table 4.1 will be briefly
reviewed and, where possible, examples from colleges will be shared.

College Commitment and Student Success

Adopting the student success practices highlighted in table 4.1 requires
college leaders to make it a priority. Community colleges operate on
tight budgets, and, by definition, innovative student success practices
require reallocation of resources. At issue is the capacity of colleges to
shift practices, resources, and the belief system of an organization that
has functioned under the access logic since inception to one that is focused on student success.

The commitment required to make this shift has been the focus of
many national conversations. The work of the American Association of
Community Colleges and the Association of Community College Trustees on the completion agenda has been designed to create the leadership
commitment and capacity necessary to make student success a priority.
Strong wording in AACC's 21st-Century Commission report directed
toward student completion along with ACCT's ongoing work with the
Governance Institute for Student Success has created a significant amount
of energy and awareness among presidents and trustees of the work that
goes into student success.[27]

How important is leadership in the completion agenda? McClenney
and Mathis argue that leadership is a key ingredient in changing the
culture of institutions and moving the completion agenda forward. There
is ample evidence to suggest that this observation is correct; however,
the scale of change necessary to effect reforms cannot happen solely as
a result of strong leadership. It requires commitment, buy-in, and active
participation from faculty and staff at all levels within colleges.[28]

Perhaps the best example of organization-wide commitment to student success can be found among colleges that have received the Aspen Prize for Community College Excellence. In 2011, the inaugural award was given to Valencia College in Florida. Based on data collected by the U.S. Department of Education, one out of two (51 percent) Valencia students graduated or transferred within three years of college enrollment. This compares to a national average of 39 percent in that same year. Similarly, in 2013 the second Aspen Prize was shared by Santa Barbara City College in California and Walla Walla Community College in Washington. These colleges had completion and transfer rates of 64 percent and 54 percent (within three years), respectively, compared to a national average of 40 percent. The 2015 Aspen Award went to Santa Fe College in Florida with a 62 percent completion/transfer rate compared to the national average of 40 percent.[29]

The Aspen Institute cited a number of reasons for strong performance among award-winning institutions, most prominent of which was a total college commitment to helping students meet individual educational goals and complete a credential. There are other examples of colleges innovating with student success not presented here. The overarching point is that it is difficult to move the success agenda at an individual institution or to realize stellar outcomes without a deep and unwavering commitment by leaders, faculty, and staff.

Use of Data to Improve Programs and Services

One of the fundamental challenges community colleges have faced since their establishment is limited analytic capacity to determine student progression, where students are experiencing difficulty, and whether or not they have completed a program. The root cause of this problem is not simply the number of staff available to do the work, although that has been a significant problem. It has more to do with the scarcity of data collected about student progress and success, underdeveloped information systems, limited interpretive ability, and a leadership culture that does not use data in decision making.

Achieving the Dream has created an expectation in the field that practitioners should rely on hard data descriptive of what is happening to students rather than anecdotal information to make decisions. ATD has pressed colleges to evaluate and strengthen their information systems, design interventions to address obstacles students were encountering, and evaluate the impact of intervention strategies.

ATD's work has enabled colleges to become increasingly sophisticated in the use of data. Early on discussion focused on data elements and metrics institutions need to track student progress and success. Building on the foundation established by ATD, organizations like the National

Center for Inquiry and Improvement and the Institute for Evidence-Based Change have emerged to work with colleges to help them move to the next level of inquiry. The question has become not just what data and metrics are needed, but also who should have access to the data and how colleges can better use data to inform dialogue among faculty, staff, and students. The ideal was and is to make instructors and front-line staff who interact with students consumers of information in accessible formats.

More recently, colleges have started to utilize predictive analytics, which employ sophisticated algorithms to predict outcomes based on historical data—specifically the likelihood that students will stop out and/or graduate based on multiple criteria. Leading the way are Sinclair Community College in Ohio, Austin Community College District in Texas, the City Colleges of Chicago, the Kentucky Community and Technical College System, and Valencia College. These institutions are working with Civitas Learning to use data science and predictive analytics as a means for improving student outcomes and enhancing learning.

Instructional Quality and Faculty Engagement

Arguably the greatest challenge of the reform movement over the past decade has been engagement of faculty in the conversation. One of the critiques of Achieving the Dream and other prominent initiatives has been that they have done everything but pull back the veil of what is happening inside classrooms and how curricula and pedagogy are contributing to student success. This critique is not without merit, but to be fair instructors see their role as helping students master the content of a particular course, not to steer them through a full program of study to graduation. This is not to say that instructors are not taking an active role in student success conversations outside of the classroom, but their unit of analysis is the courses they teach and the students in front of them. Changing this culture is an important part of the conversation about completion, but to be effective faculty engagement must be authentic, meaningful, and sustained over time.

One method of faculty engagement that has caught on at colleges across the country is faculty inquiry groups. Inquiry groups are a form of collaborative professional development where faculty come together in small groups, identify a question about student learning, and work as a team to formulate an answer. As part of a project titled Strengthening Pre-Collegiate Education and Community Colleges, the Carnegie Foundation for the Advancement of Teaching launched a multiyear effort using inquiry groups as a basis for discussion about improving the delivery of developmental education.[30]

Prominent in the area of discussion about developmental education curriculum and instruction are strategies to accelerate the delivery of remedial content. The goal of the acceleration strategies is to mitigate problems created by the long sequences of developmental coursework, but these strategies also better align developmental courses with college-level curricula. Three often cited examples of developmental acceleration strategies are FastStart at the Community College of Denver, Accelerated English at Chabot College in California, and the Accelerated Learning Program (ALP) at the Community College of Baltimore County.

In each instance, programs are designed to shorten the sequence of developmental courses, thereby eliminating opportunities for students to stop out. The FastStart program pairs developmental math courses in the same term. The accelerated developmental English option at Chabot allows students select between a single development course and the traditional two-course sequence before enrolling in college-level English. The ALP model is a co-requisite model in which students who would otherwise place into the highest developmental writing course are instead placed in the college-level course and provided with supplemental instruction. The Community College Research Center recently produced an excellent brief summarizing research about accelerated programs. A common outcome of accelerated programs was higher rates of sequential course enrollment and completion among students who took the accelerated option in math, English, and writing.[31]

Accelerated development education programs are being modeled at colleges throughout the nation. The question is whether or not students are enrolling in accelerated options if they are available to them. According to recent surveys conducted by the Center for Community College Student Engagement (CCCSE), less than 30 percent of students in developmental education are participating in accelerated course options, despite the fact that 70 percent of colleges offer them.[32] Given positive outcomes of the models described earlier it is not surprising that policymakers are pressing for accelerated developmental education—a point we'll revisit later in the chapter.

Streamlined Pathways to Credentials and Careers

Much of state policy dialogue about completion rates has been on alignment (or the lack thereof) among K–12, community colleges, adult basic education, universities, workforce development, and labor market demand. Partnering with high schools and adult education providers locally, community colleges have sought to smooth on ramps to enrollment. They have created dual enrollment programs to meet growing demand from students and parents seeking an opportunity to gain college credit while in high school. Similarly, depending on the state, colleges have developed a litany of transfer and articulation agreements with universities to help students transfer more easily to the four-year institution of their choice. These are important steps, but there is a conversation that has emerged as part of the completion agenda that is even more important: Is the alignment of curricula between community colleges and other sectors sufficient to ensure seamless transition to a career or additional education?

A number of researchers have suggested that colleges need to create greater clarity around the programs of study students pursue.[33] Jenkins and Cho's research suggests that students should enter a defined program of study as early as possible. They found that students "who do not enter a program within a year of enrollment are far less likely to ever enter a program and, therefore, are less likely to earn a credential."[34] The point of many of these studies is to better understand when and where students fall out of the system, identify interventions to fix the problem, and streamline the overall student experience. This research is the conceptual underpinning of prominent national initiatives around guided or structured pathways.

The most prominent of these efforts has been the Completion by Design initiative funded by the Bill and Melinda Gates Foundation. Initiated in 2011, Completion by Design involved clusters of colleges in three states (Florida, North Carolina, and Ohio) to design and implement systemic changes in policies, programs, and practices to strengthen pathways to completion for students on their campuses. Participating colleges in this initiative were Miami Dade College in Florida; Guilford Technical, Central Piedmont, Davidson County, Martin, and Wake Technical Community Colleges in North Carolina; and Sinclair, Lorain County, and Stark State Community Colleges in Ohio. Each college received substantial financial and technical support for institutional redesign. There were also partner organizations in each state helping to support state policy dialogues stemming from the colleges' experience with redesign as well as developing mechanisms for scaling lessons learned to other institutions.

The Completion by Design initiative was based on a four-part "loss-momentum" framework that focused on the full student experience with community college from initial *connection* and interest to application, the process for college *entry* through completion of program gatekeeper courses, *progress* made from program entry to completion of program requirements, and *completion* of a credential of value for further education and labor market advancement. The goal was to speed up the process of program entry, map and clearly articulate programs, and redesign and integrate college advising, monitoring, and student support systems to keep students on the path to completion.[35]

The work of the Completion by Design colleges and states has spurred a significant amount of interest in replicating guided pathways conversations in other states. Several states not involved in Completion by Design have established Student Success Centers to support the completion efforts of community colleges and most are based on the guided pathways approach. Similarly, Complete College America, which is focused largely on policy, is seeking to support states that are interested in spurring guided pathways discussion with colleges. Most recently researchers from the Community College Research Center published *Redesigning America's Community Colleges*,[36] which provides a compelling case for the guided pathways approach. Drawing on CCRC's work, the American Association of Community Colleges launched the Pathways Project in 2016 with funding from the Bill and Melinda Gates Foundation to focus on scaling guided pathways principles to thirty colleges throughout the nation.

Ongoing Advising and Monitoring Student Progression

This category of practice is focused on college efforts to provide sufficient resources for core advising to ensure adequate ratios between advisors and students, streamline bureaucratic processes, and implement mandatory advising and orientation programs. Regular surveys conducted at colleges across the country by the CCCSE have yielded robust information from students, faculty, and staff about high-impact student success practices. Among the thirteen high-impact practices CCCSE profiled in *A Matter of Degrees: Practices to Pathways*, two fall into the advising and monitoring category of practice: academic goal setting and planning and orientation.[37]

CCCSE suggests that orientation can be a single two-hour session with incoming students, a semester-long student success course, or some combination of both. Regardless of how it is structured, colleges use orientation to help students acquire information they must have before classes begin. CCCSE's 2013 report highlighted the work of Tallahassee Community College (TCC) in Florida to improve orientation by offering both a full-day and a half-day option for students. TCC also gave students the option of attending alone or having a parent join them. The college found that students who attended the full-day session were more likely to enroll in the next term than students who only attended the half-day session. Students who attended orientation with a parent were also more likely to reenroll in the next term than those who came by themselves.[38]

The other category of practice profiled by CCCSE worth noting here is academic goal setting and planning. Drawing on principles embedded in Completion by Design, goal setting and planning are about more than simply choosing classes. They are about articulating goals that students have defined and a path toward achievement. CCCSE found that less than half of students surveyed develop an academic plan during their first term, even though two-thirds of colleges have a process for doing so. Zane State College in Ohio has instituted an intrusive advising program that builds on a "personal touch" philosophy about interaction with students. Zane's advising model includes mandatory meetings, emails, and Facebook postings that not only build a connection with students, but also allow college staff to remind students of other services that are available. The results have been striking with fall-to-fall retention rates for at-risk students increasing 11 percent on average over a five-year period.[39]

From the early days of Achieving the Dream, orientation and advising have been areas of significant work by participating colleges as key strategies for improving student progress and success. According to the Achieving the Dream Interventions Showcase, forty-seven colleges have implemented new orientation programs and seventy-four colleges have enhanced advising programs and systems to better support students. Again this discussion is through the lens of specific national initiatives and programs; undoubtedly there is a substantial amount of activity quietly underway on college campuses that is not captured here.[40]

Integrated Student Supports and Services

Much like the practices described earlier, integrated student supports and services are intended to help students get started on the right track and stay on course toward completion. Integrated student services are designed to mesh with academic affairs and include student success (or life skill) courses that are optional for some students but mandatory for students needing academic remediation. Learning communities and paired courses to establish cohort learning illustrate how student development and academic affairs can come together to shape practice around student needs. Early warning and intrusive advising systems serve as additional support for at-risk students that enable instructors and student services staff to promptly address issues that retard student progress.

The Achieving the Dream Interventions Showcase indicates that seventy-eight colleges in the network have engaged in work focused on the first-year experience. An additional sixty colleges have designed new student success courses, twenty-nine colleges have developed new learning community interventions for at-risk students, and thirty-eight colleges have created supplemental instruction programs for students placing into developmental education.[41]

Survey research conducted by CCCSE has revealed that 60 percent of colleges offer some semblance of a first-year experience program, but less than 30 percent of the students actually participate. A similarly disconcerting pattern emerged from CCCSE's analysis of student success courses. Fewer than 30 percent of students surveyed indicated that they took the student success course during their first term of enrollment despite the fact that 84 percent of the colleges surveyed offered this option to students. Kay McClenney, former director of the Center for Community College Student Engagement, has often remarked that "students don't do optional." If colleges don't make proven interventions and practices mandatory, students will not avail themselves of the opportunity. The data cited here confirm this observation and provides a strong argument for seamless integration of student services and academic programs in which students are enrolled.[42]

The City University of New York's (CUNY) Accelerated Study and Associate Program (ASAP), launched in 2007 at Borough of Manhattan, Kingsborough, and LaGuardia community colleges in CUNY, offers a powerful example of how integrated programs can have a dramatic impact on student outcomes. ASAP is a comprehensive program that requires students to attend full time, encourages them enroll in and complete developmental courses early, and to graduate within three years. Students in the program receive systemic advising including enhanced career guidance with an advisor who has a small caseload. The colleges participating in this program offer blocked or linked courses in the first year as well as a student success course in the first few semesters. Financially, the program offers waivers for tuition if there are any gaps between financial aid and the cost of attendance. It also offers free access to public transportation and free textbooks, as long as students participate in other features of the program.

A recent study by MDRC indicates that the ASAP program had been effectively implemented and communicated to students with clear expectations. In terms of outcomes, MDRC found that students participating in ASAP earn a significantly higher number of credits in three years compared with those who are not enrolled in the program. Over the course of the study, 40 percent of the students enrolled in the program had received a degree, compared to 22 percent of those who didn't participate in ASAP. Additionally, 25 percent of the students in ASAP enrolled in a four-year college or university compared to 17 percent of those not enrolled in the program. One of the critiques of integrated programs is the cost associated with running them. MDRC found at the end of the three-year study that the cost per degree for ASAP students was lower than the control group in large part because more students graduated.[43] This is a particularly promising finding as institutions seek to understand the return on investment in integrated programs.

EMERGING CONSENSUS AMONG STATE POLICY INITIATIVES

With considerable investment and advocacy on the part of educational foundations, policymakers in many states have moved aggressively to adopt policies to create conditions and incentives to improve the rate at which students attain credentials. The following pages discuss these efforts through the lens of philanthropic policy initiatives. The specifics of these initiatives are varied, but most focus on performance funding and measurement systems, efforts to align educational systems around college readiness and transfer dialogues, and direct involvement in curricula through policies advocating redesign or elimination of developmental education.

It is worth reiterating that federal policy has played a crucial role in framing the completion agenda. In addition to the bold completion goals President Obama has set forth, programs and initiatives have been proposed that have directed attention to many of the issues examined in this book. However, the fact remains that public colleges and universities are largely governed and influenced by state policy. In recognition of this dynamic, the discussion of policy in this section is limited to what has been happening at the state level.

Table 4.2 highlights broad categories of policies that have been adopted over the past decade with the intent of improving completion rates. The table is organized around policy "buckets" of the College Completion Toolkit, created by the U.S. Department of Education as a means to articulate strategies governors should consider when promoting college completion. This toolkit is keyed to state policy reforms that emerged through Achieving the Dream's State Policy Network managed by Jobs for the Future, Complete College America, the Strategy Labs created by the Lumina Foundation, and other related state policy initiatives.[44]

Table 4.2. State Policy Strategies to Increase Completion

Strategy
1 Set college completion goals and develop an action plan
2 Embrace performance-based funding of higher education based on progress toward completion and other quality goals
3 Align high school graduation, workforce training, and adult education expectations to public college admission and placement requirements
4 Make it easier for students to transfer among colleges
5 Use data to drive decision making
6 Accelerate learning, reduce costs, and stabilize tuition growth
7 Target adults, especially those with "some college but no degree"

Source: Adapted from U.S. Department of Education. U.S. Department of Education, *College Completion Toolkit* (Washington, DC: U.S. Dept. of Ed., 2011).

Set Goals and Develop an Action Plan

The first step for state policymakers as part of the completion agenda is setting a state-level educational attainment goal. It is difficult to mobilize constituents to action without an end goal; it is no different for policymakers when it comes to student outcomes and educational attainment. A 2014 report issued by the National Center for Higher Education Management Systems (NCHEMS) articulated state policies related to attainment goals and the completion agenda. Prominent among the findings in this report was that twenty-six states have a statewide attainment goal and ten more were in the process of setting a goal. Looking more closely at the individual state goals, many if not most reflect a derivative of the Lumina Foundation's "big goal" that by 2025 60 percent of Americans between the ages of twenty-five and sixty-four will hold a college degree, certificate, or high-quality postsecondary credential. Some states like Kentucky, Colorado, Massachusetts, and Washington target a narrower age range to increase attainment. Other states like Delaware, Idaho, Nevada, Utah, and Vermont set goals with a shorter time horizon than Lumina.[45]

Regardless of the specifics of each state's completion goal, the more important question is if states have action plans to achieve the goal. The report from NCHEMS explored the manner in which completion goals are attached to policy levers such as funding formulas, alignment between education sectors, financial aid policy, etc. Of the states with goals in place or in process, twenty-one have linked completion levels and funding, and forty-two states are linking other policies to completion. In this way, states are actively using attainment goals to drive policy decisions and ultimately institutional behavior.

As part of the work of national completion initiatives focused on policy (that is, Achieving the Dream State Policy Network and Complete College America), state agencies engaged in completion efforts have been required to assess their policy context compared to other states, identify gaps or deficiencies in state statutes and administrative rules, and create action plans to strengthen their policy environment. Depending on the state, action plans have focused on administrative rules, legislative change, or, more recently, venues for colleges to learn from one another. Complete College America (CCA) has taken the completion agenda a step further. Not only did CCA require participating states to develop a statewide plan, it has also pushed the states to ensure that institutions create plans for increasing completion as well.

Embrace Performance-Based Funding

The underlying assumption of many policymakers is that college behavior will not change unless incentives are changed. Accordingly, policymakers and foundations have pressed for changes in the way institutions are funded. State support for higher education has historically been based on inputs—that is, enrollments. While this approach to funding has facilitated access to postsecondary education, it has not had a favorable effect on completion. If policymakers want to increase the number of degrees and certificates, the growing consensus is that they will need to focus on outcomes as the basis for funding. This is the fundamental principle that has culminated in thirty-five states adopting outcomes-based funding formulas that reward institutions for the number of students that progress toward and complete a degree.

A 2015 report titled *Driving Better Outcomes* articulated a typology and principles approaches to implementing outcomes-based funding. States identified in the report as exhibiting strength in outcomes-based funding employ criteria such as connecting the funding formula to state attainment goals, maintaining stable funding, tying a significant percentage of money to outcomes, customizing funding to different sectors of postsecondary institutions, and prioritizing the success of underrepresented student groups. In the report, the authors highlight Ohio and Tennessee as "exemplar" states because of the amount of base funding tied to outcomes, 100 percent and 85 percent, respectively, but also because of the sophistication of the funding models.[46]

Interestingly, of the states that have adopted outcomes-based funding formulas, only five states have devoted more than 10 percent of institutional funding to these formulas. Among the remaining states, five allocate between 5 and 10 percent and the balance allocates less than 5 percent to outcomes-based funding. One of the critiques of outcomes-based funding is that not enough money is devoted to it to influence institutional behavior. This analysis certainly suggests that most states are not yet willing to tie substantial funding to institutional outcomes. This may change as more evidence emerges about the impact these outcomes-based funding models have on student outcomes.[47]

It is important to make a distinction between variants of performance funding that were prevalent before 2005 and those that have emerged over the past decade. Under "performance funding 1.0"—the prominent funding mechanism before 2005—additional state funds were made available to institutions above base appropriations. These funds were targeted to specific initiatives such as enhancing access (that is, lower tuition) at open-admissions colleges or incentives for universities to promote research commercialization. Because added dollars were on top of base institutional funding, they were vulnerable in economic downturns when states needed to cut budgets. Overall these models provided relatively small amounts of funding to institutions and, not surprisingly, research on "performance funding 1.0 models" found negligible impact.

In contrast, performance funding 2.0—the approach described earlier— tied institutional base funding directly to student progress and outcomes. Kevin Dougherty, who has studied performance funding for over a decade, released a series of papers in November 2014 examining the adoption, implementation, and impact of the performance funding models in

Indiana, Ohio, and Tennessee. The primary finding of Dougherty's work is that it is difficult to discern the specific impact of outcomes-based funding because the amount of time that has passed since the models were adopted is too short to permit adequate measurement. Dougherty also notes that the bevy of completion initiatives underway at colleges make it difficult to isolate the effect of funding formulas. Interviews conducted with policymakers and practitioners suggested that colleges are responding to funding model incentives by altering policies and procedures; however, states are doing very little to help colleges build capacity to make needed changes.[48]

Align High School Standards with College Entrance and Placement Standards

A prominent obstacle to improving success rates has been the number of students enrolling in postsecondary education who are not ready for college-level coursework. As noted previously, college readiness has been a major focal point for most, if not all, national initiatives. In terms of state policy, there have been a variety of activities to address this problem, including strategies to alleviate the need for remediation, helping colleges do a better job placing students in developmental courses, and incentivizing colleges to accelerate students to college-level courses.

By definition, preventing students from requiring remediation would require them to be college ready upon enrolling in a community college. The primary focus of work directed at remedial prevention over the past decade has been efforts to ensure more students leave high school ready for college. The discussion about college readiness in many states predates the completion agenda. However, over the past decade state efforts to improve college readiness have been eclipsed by the national effort led by the Council of Chief State School Officers and National Governors Association to establish Common Core State Standards.

Despite controversy concerning the federal role in the Common Core, education chiefs and governors in most states have adopted Common Core standards. The standards are intended to serve as goals for what students should know and be able to do at each grade level. The intent is that they will help teachers ensure that their students have the skills and knowledge necessary to succeed and that parents will know what is expected of children. Currently forty-three states are working to implement Common Core standards using nationally developed assessments. Two state-led consortia—the Partnership for Assessment of Readiness for College and Careers (PARCC) and the Smarter Balanced Assessment Consortium (Smarter Balanced)—have been working with states to develop, pilot, and implement tests aligned to the Common Core. Most states are participating in one of these consortia and assessments were to be available in the 2014–15 school year.

Another important strategy to eliminate the need for developmental education is the early assessment and remediation during high school. California and Florida are examples of states that have adopted proactive policies to create partnerships between community colleges and high schools to implement this strategy. Students are tested in eleventh grade to determine if they are college ready. If they are deemed college ready, they circumvent placement tests upon enrolling in a community college as long as they enroll within an allotted amount of time. Students that are not college ready receive additional instruction in twelfth grade to remediate deficiencies. The models for delivering twelfth-grade interventions vary. In some instances, it is high school teachers providing additional instruction based on the college curriculum. In other instances, it is college faculty providing instruction to twelfth-grade students.

In addition to early assessment, several states have sought to reform the way developmental education is delivered. For example, Texas and Virginia have promoted statewide approaches to reframing developmental education. Virginia has focused on modularized content involving smaller chunks of developmental education delivered in shorter periods of time than a full semester. Virginia has developed a diagnostic assessment designed to provide a fine-grained picture of the content students lack.

Texas community colleges are working collaboratively to implement the New Mathways Project in partnership with the Charles A. Dana Center at the University of Texas at Austin. This project is designed to create multiple pathways with mathematics content aligned to specific fields of study. Like other acceleration strategies, the intent of the pathways is to move students more quickly toward completion of a college-level math course than would be possible with the traditional developmental math sequence. In both Texas and Virginia, the developmental education reform efforts have been informed by research and strategies have been adopted on a collaborative basis among colleges in each state.

The efforts in Texas and Virginia to reform developmental education stand in stark contrast to recent initiatives in Connecticut and Florida, where the delivery and effectiveness of developmental education has become an issue in the legislature. In Connecticut, the legislature mandated a limit on how many remedial courses students can take. In Florida, the legislature prohibited community colleges from requiring students to take a placement test or to enroll in developmental courses.

The effect of these legislative decrees has been met with concern by colleges as they attempt to react to a changing public policy environment. In both states, the legislature is focused on how developmental education is delivered rather than underlying reasons why it is necessary to begin with. There is no question that research points to problems with the structure and delivery of developmental education. However, to ignore student remedial needs and to prohibit meaningful interventions by institutions simply returns us to an environment in which students have a "right to fail." Time will tell what the impact of these legislative actions will be, but it is likely that if there is not thoughtful dialogue about students needing academic remediation, many students may simply fall out of the system.

Make Transfer Easier for Students

Recent studies by the National Student Clearinghouse (NSC) indicate that students are increasingly mobile between postsecondary institutions as they pursue a degree. For example, in a recent report examining student transfer and mobility, NSC found that one-third of enrolled students transferred at least once within five years, with the most common time of transfer being the second year. Citing evidence that is counterintuitive to many conversations about transfer, NSC also found that the most common destination for transferring students was a public two-year college regardless of where they started. These data indicate that mobility patterns are more complex than the traditional notion of vertical transfer from a community college to a university. This also suggests that institutions need to be thinking about how to support transfer students regardless of whether an institution is sending or receiving students.[49]

The mobility of students coupled with the rising cost of higher education has led policymakers to look for ways to streamline transitions between institutions and to minimize the number of credit hours and courses not accepted and in need of repetition. In a recent report on state responses to increased student mobility among higher education institutions, the Education Commission of the States found that states are moving away from "fragmented transfer policies set by individual institutions" to a coherent approach to transfer and articulation among colleges and universities.

Examples of state policy changes and the number of states that have adopted them include statewide common course numbering (fifteen states), statewide credit by assessment (sixteen states), statewide guaranteed transfer of the associate degree (thirty-seven states), and statewide transferable lower-division core courses (thirty-five states). While state adoption and implementation policies vary in specifics, the overarching theme is that states are becoming more prescriptive about transfer and acceptance of credits by receiving colleges and universities.[50]

State efforts to reform transfer and articulation policies are closely related to the idea of guided or structured programmatic pathways that are underway at a growing number of institutions. As noted in the discussion about streamlining pathways, institutions need to be more aware of the full student experience from entry to completion and to a job or further education. Programmatic pathways within colleges and how these pathways intersect with transition between institutions are of critical importance to transfer policy.

College "A" can do a wonderful job developing programs and curricula, guiding students into them, and monitoring and supporting student success. However, if programs at College "A" are transfer-oriented (nonterminal) and there isn't a clear process for articulating credits to University "B" such that the credits are not only accepted but also applied to a baccalaureate degree, the student will end up having to repeat credits at personal expense and expense to the system. It is this scenario that state transfer policy is attempting to mitigate.

The Education Commission of the States released a report in 2014 indicating that eighteen states had enacted or considered legislation focused on guided pathways for students. More recently, the Community College Research Center, the Aspen Institute, and the National Student Clearinghouse partnered on a report titled *Tracking Transfer: New Measures of Institutional and State Effectiveness in Helping Community College Students Attain Bachelor's Degrees*, advancing new metrics, describing how institutional characteristics impact performance on these metrics, and how states perform overall. This and other research is shedding light on variations in state and institutional performance that will undoubtedly influence policy discussions moving forward.[51]

Use Data to Drive Decision Making

Much like the discussion of the use of data by individual colleges, the capacity across states relative to the availability and use of data varies widely. Without reliable data, state leaders are handicapped in developing the right mix of policy initiatives to advance the completion agenda. To remedy these issues, states have worked aggressively to enhance their data capacity and methods to share information with policymakers, key constituents, and the general public. More specifically, states have focused on developing longitudinal data systems and robust metrics to gauge educational performance.

A challenge policymakers face as they consider methods for improving completion rates in their states is a substantial gap in the information available about students. Much of the early framing of the completion agenda has been focused on student progression through the educational pipeline. Dialogue about the pipeline requires longitudinal data on student progress and cannot simply be viewed via snapshots in time. This gap has spurred significant interest in the development of unit record data systems at the state level[52] that can track individual students over time by linking preschool, K–12, adult education, postsecondary education, and workforce development data.

A prominent player in this space on the national level has been the Data Quality Campaign (DQC), a nonprofit organization supporting efforts of state policymakers and key leaders to promote the effective use of data to improve student achievement. For the past decade, DQC has provided technical assistance for states developing longitudinal data systems and tracked the adoption of these systems across the nation. While much of this work is technical in nature, significant progress has been made in a relatively short time.

In 2005 only twelve states had the capability to match student-level P–12 and higher education data. By 2011, this number had increased to forty-nine states. A critical piece that has been slower to develop is the matching of education data with labor market outcomes information. If we are to have a better understanding of the value of certificates and degrees in the labor market, we will need to connect the dots between programs completed and jobs students ultimately acquire. Based on DQC's most recent survey of states, nineteen states could match these records. This is up from eleven states in 2011. Early adopters of this capability include Arkansas, Florida, North Carolina, Texas, and Washington.[53]

Another major development in terms of data use at the state level has been the creation of metrics to gauge the performance of colleges. Many states have developed performance metrics and share them in accessible dashboards to inform policymakers and the general public. Several national initiatives have sought to influence the type of performance metrics states (and colleges) use. These initiatives include the American Association of Community Colleges's Voluntary Framework of Accountability, Complete College America's Complete to Compete project in partnership with the National Governors Association, and Achieving the Dream's Cross-State Data Work Group. States that have contributed substantially to the dialogue on performance metrics are California, Connecticut, Florida, North Carolina, Ohio, Texas, Virginia, and Washington.

Common to national initiatives is the inclusion of intermediate and final success measures. Intermediate metrics capture critical events such as successful completion of developmental education and/or college-level gatekeeper courses, credit accumulation in the first term and/or first year, fall-to-spring and fall-to-fall retention, and course completion. The emergence of intermediate milestones has helped states and institutions think more proactively about interventions and policies needed to help students progress. Without these transitional metrics, policymakers and practitioners would be left solely with final outcomes information, which is important but of limited utility in policy initiatives without information about progression.

The success metrics included in national discussions include graduation rates, transfer rates, number (and percentage) of degrees and certificates awarded, time to degree, and credits to degree. Another set of outcome metrics that should be included in this list relates to labor market outcomes (for example, job placement in field of study and wage growth of graduates), but, as noted earlier, metrics of this type require the ability to match education and labor data.

The emergence of longitudinal data systems and new metrics measuring student progression and completion has significantly enhanced the quality of information available to policymakers and the public. The extent to which this information is being effectively used is variable, and states will need to invest in human capacity to ensure that information is leveraged. The Bill and Melinda Gates Foundation has recently funded work with the Institute for Higher Education Policy (IHEP) and the State Higher Education Executive Officers to continue efforts to bring coherence and innovation to performance measurement and data use. Early outcomes of this initiative have been a set of eleven papers published by IHEP—*Envisioning the National Postsecondary Infrastructure in the 21st Century*—aimed at improving national postsecondary data systems.[54]

Accelerate Learning and Reduce Costs

One of the major themes of the completion agenda in general and state policy dialogues in particular has been the need to accelerate student progress through academic programs. The root cause of this focus stems from two factors. One is that research suggests that the longer it takes students to complete a degree program, the less likely they are to do so. The second factor is the notion that the education system is inefficient and causing undue costs to taxpayers, students, and families.

There are a number of strategies that have been explored and implemented to accelerate learning and reduce costs. They include dual enrollment models, methods for accelerated delivery of developmental education, streamlining credit articulation between postsecondary institutions, assessing and awarding credit for life experience and/or military service, mechanisms for pushing students to take heavier course loads, and limiting the number of credits required for a credential.

Accelerated developmental education and improved transfer and articulation policies have already been discussed. Both dual enrollment and prior learning assessments are important strategies for shortening the time it takes students to earn a postsecondary credential, but there are complexities involved with each. In both instances the goal is to move students farther faster toward a degree. Dual enrollment and prior learning assessments have strong support among policymakers and reform-minded practitioners because they offer seemingly intuitive solutions to a vexing issue, but they have detractors as well because of implementation issues and financial implications.

Increasing student credit hour loads and limiting the number of credit hours required for a degree are increasingly prominent strategies that policymakers are using to accelerate student progress. Complete College America (CCA) has aggressively sought to encourage governors and state legislators to adopt accelerated learning and reduction of time to degree strategies. Since its launch in 2009, CCA has focused on strategies to improve completion rates, but the overarching theme of their work is acceleration of time to completion. In a 2011 report titled *Time is the Enemy*, CCA used data from thirty-plus states in their network to highlight time to degree. Despite the moniker of a two-year degree, full-time students averaged 3.8 years to complete an associate degree and part-time students took five years to complete the same degree.[55]

Conducting similar analyses for students completing certificates and baccalaureate degrees, CCA found that one of the primary reasons underlying extended time to completion was the excessive number of credits student take before completing a credential. Looking at students who were pursuing an associate degree in their network states, CCA found that students earned on average seventy-nine credits before completing a two-year degree that should only require sixty credits. These data provide a compelling account of why only 18.8 percent of full-time students complete an associate degree within four years and only 7.8 percent of part-time students finish in the same time period. CCA has used this report to advocate for state-level policy, including implementation of outcomes-based funding, reform of developmental education, and adoption of guided pathways with structured schedules.[56]

CCA has also encouraged institutions and states to adopt policy that would define full-time attendance as fifteen credit hours per semester rather than twelve credit hours, which is the federal definition for financial aid purposes. In a subsequent report titled *Four-Year Myth*, CCA highlights the problem of small numbers of students completing a degree on time. There are a variety of reasons why completion is delayed, but a compelling factor is that students who attend full time take only twelve credits per semester and are immediately behind timely completion of a degree. In theory, an associate degree for a full-time student taking fifteen credits per semester should take two years and a bachelor's degree would take twice that time.[57]

As these statistics indicate, reality says otherwise. In response to this challenge, a national campaign has been launched called "15 to finish."

At present, fifteen states ranging from Colorado to Hawaii and Illinois to Texas have signed on to this campaign and are adopting legislation and/or administrative policies that push full-time students to take fifteen credit hours per semester.

Target Adults, Especially Those with Some College but no Degree

As noted in chapter 1, there have been several national initiatives in the past decade—Bridges to Opportunity, Breaking Through, and Accelerating Opportunity—designed to bring about changes in state policy and college practice that promote educational opportunities for low-income adults. These initiatives focus on helping colleges advance low-skilled adults into careers through strategies that accelerate learning, provide comprehensive supports, and incorporate course content that has a labor market payoff. They also seek to rectify misalignment of systems designed to support adults with low basic skills and to change the delivery of Adult Basic Education (ABE) by integrating basic skills education and credit-bearing career technical/occupational programs leading to employment. The goal of this ongoing work is to make ABE an on ramp for students to enter and complete postsecondary education and move on to family-supporting careers.

In addition to efforts targeting adults with low basic skills, a number of states have sought to identity adults who have some college but no degree and mobilize them to reenroll and finish the credential they started. A recent study by the National Student Clearinghouse examined the population of adults with some college but no degree, and they found that over a ten-year period (2003–2013) there were more than 3.5 million individuals who had accrued two or more years of academic progress based on enrollment records. This suggests that there are a large number of adults who could conceivably return to finish postsecondary degrees in a relatively short period of time—an enticing population for practitioners, foundations, and policymakers to target as low-hanging fruit for degree completion.[58]

Policy efforts in this area track two national initiatives such as Project Win-Win and Credit When It's Due. Project Win-Win targets students who have accumulated a significant number of credits but are no longer enrolled at any institution and have not received a credential. The intent is to encourage these students to return to college and finish the credits they need to complete a degree.

In 2013 a summary of Project Win-Win published by the Institute for Higher Education Policy reported that sixty-one institutions across nine states were able to award 6,218 associate degrees. Learners completing a degree came from an initial pool of 128,614 former students colleges identified as degree eligible and then attempted to reconnect with. Using National Student Clearinghouse data, participating colleges were able to determine that 86,925, or 68 percent, of the initial pool were enrolled in another institution or had received a degree elsewhere. Of the 47,710 remaining students, colleges were able to locate and award a degree to 13 percent of them.[59]

Given the success of recent initiatives with adult learners, policymakers have intensified efforts to support outreach to "near completers." Policy efforts in this area have taken the form of grant programs to institutions such as the One Step Away State Grant in Maryland, intended to support college and university efforts to identify and mobilize noncompleting populations to degree completion. Florida has employed a similar approach, but has also passed legislation impelling institutions to use prior learning assessments to fill the gap between credits students have accumulated and those required to complete a degree.

Credit When It's Due is a national initiative focused on students transferring to a university prior to associate degree completion. The goal of this initiative is to encourage students to "reverse transfer" credits to the community college that will satisfy outstanding requirements so the associate degree can be retroactively awarded. This initiative is ongoing, but among the fifteen states involved, six have been helped by legislation to promote reverse transfer.

According to a report by a research partner of the Office of Community College Research and Leadership at the University of Illinois, the language employed in legislation in some states (Michigan and Florida) simply encourages colleges and universities to develop partnerships to promote reverse transfer, while other states charge the state higher education coordinating agency to develop statewide policies and procedures—specifically Colorado, Maryland, Missouri, and Oregon. These national initiatives and the state policies that have accompanied them have played out in a variety of ways in states and institutions as policymakers and practitioners look for easier ways to increase attainment by targeting students who have made progress toward a degree.[60]

The state policy actions discussed in this chapter closely parallel the interventions and strategies individual colleges have been implementing under the label of the completion agenda. The research discussed in the first part of the chapter has provided the conceptual and empirical underpinning for activity at both the institutional and state levels. While there is synergy between research, practice, and policy, there are still gaps that, if left unaddressed, could have significant unintended consequences for the effectiveness of reform efforts, the quality of instruction provided, and access to postsecondary education for students from underrepresented backgrounds. The next chapter will explore presidential perspectives on the challenge of completion as well as opportunities the completion agenda presents.

NOTES

1. Steven Brint and Jerome Karabel, *The Diverted Dream: Community Colleges and the Promise of Educational Opportunity in America, 1900–1985* (New York: Oxford University Press, 1989); Burton R. Clark, "The 'Cooling Out' Function in Higher Education," *American Journal of Sociology* 65, no. 6 (1960): 569–76; Steven Brint, "Few Remaining Dreams: Community Colleges since 1985," *Annals of the American Academy of Political and Social Science* 586 (2003): 16–37.

2. James E. Rosenbaum, Regina Deil-Amen, and Ann E Person, *After Admission: From College Access to College Success* (New York: Russell Sage Foundation, 2006); Peter R. Bahr, "Classifying Community Colleges Based on Students' Pattern of Use," *Research in Higher Education* 54 (2013): 433–60.

3. Mariana Alfonso, "The Impact of Community College Attendance on Baccalaureate Attainment," *Research in Higher Education* 47 (2006): 873–903; Therese L. Baker and William Velez, "Access to and Opportunity in Postsecondary Education in the United States: A Review," *Sociology of Education* 69 (1996): 82–101; Kevin J. Dougherty, "Community Colleges and Baccalaureate Attainment," *The Journal of Higher Education* 63, no. 2 (1992): 188; Bridgett Terry Long and Michael Kurlaender, "Do Community Colleges Provide a Viable Pathway to a Baccalaureate Degree?" *Educational Evaluation and Policy Analysis* 31, no. 1 (2009): 30–53; Cecilia Elena Rouse, "Do Two-Year Colleges Increase Overall Educational Attainment? Evidence from the States," *Journal of Policy Analysis and Management* 17, no. 4 (1998): 595–620.

4. Alfonso, "The Impact of Community College Attendance on Baccalaureate Attainment"; Terry Ishitani, "How Do Transfers Survive After 'Transfer Shock'? A Longitudinal Study of Transfer Student Departure at a Four-Year Institution," *Research in Higher Education* 49 (2008): 403–19; Tatiana Melguizo and Alicia C. Dowd, "Baccalaureate Success of Transfers and Rising 4-Year College Juniors," *Teachers College Record* 111, no. 1 (2009): 55–89; Xueli Wang, "Baccalaureate Attainment and College Persistence of Community College Transfer Students at Four-Year Institutions," *Research in Higher Education* 50 (2009): 570–588; Josipa Roksa, "Does the Vocational Focus of Community Colleges Hinder Student's Educational Attainment?" *The Review of Higher Education* 29, no. 4 (2006): 499–526.

5. Duane E. Leigh and Andrew M. Gill, "Do Community Colleges Really Divert Students from Earning Bachelor's Degrees?" *Economics of Education Review* 22 (2003): 23–30; Roksa, "Does the Vocational Focus of Community Colleges Hinder Student's Educational Attainment?"

6. Brint and Karabel, *The Diverted Dream*; Roksa, "Does the Vocational Focus of Community Colleges Hinder Student's Educational Attainment?"

7. David B. Monaghan and Paul Attewell, "The Community College Route to the Bachelor's Degree," *Educational Evaluation and Policy Analysis* 371 (2014): 70–91.

8. Regina Deil-Amen and James E. Rosenbaum, "The Social Prerequisites of Success: Can College Structure Reduce the Need for Social Know-How?" *Annals of the American Academy of Political and Social Science* 586 (2003): 120–43, 120.

9. Brent D. Cejda and Jay Leist, "Challenges Facing Community Colleges: Perceptions of Chief Academic Officers in Nine States," *Community College Journal of Research and Practice* 30 (2006): 253–74; Stephen J. Handel and Eileen Strempel, *Transition and Transformation: Fostering Transfer Student Success* (Dahlonega, GA:

University of North Georgia Press, 2016); Ishitani, "How Do Transfers Survive After 'Transfer Shock?'"

10. Doug Shapiro, Afet Dundar, Mary Ziskin, Yi-Chen Chiang, Jin Chen, Autumn Harrell, and Vasti Torres, *Baccalaureate Attainment: A National View of the Postsecondary Outcomes of Students Who Transfer from Two-Year to Four-Year Institutions* (Herndon, VA: National Student Clearinghouse Research Center, 2006).

11. David Crook, Colin C. Chellman, and Aleksandra Holod, *Does Earning an Associate Degree Lead to Better Baccalaureate Outcomes for Transfer Students?* (New York: Office of Policy Research, The City University of New York, 2012); Peter M. Crosta and Elizabeth Kopko, "Should Community College Students Earn an Associate Degree Before Transferring to a 4-Year Institution?" *Research in Higher Education* 57 (2015): 190–222.

12. Shanna Smith Jaggars and Georgia West Stacey, *What We Know About Developmental Education Outcomes* (New York: Community College Research Center, Teachers College, Columbia University, 2014).

13. Ibid.

14. Ibid.

15. Peter Riley Bahr, "The Aftermath of Remedial Math: Investigating the Low Rate of Certificate Completion among Remedial Math Students," *Research in Higher Education* 54, no. 2 (2013): 171–200; Thomas Bailey, Dong Wook Jeong, and Sung-Woo Cho, "Referral, Enrollment, and Completion in Developmental Education Sequences in Community Colleges," *Economics of Education Review* 29, no. 2 (2010): 255–70; Eric Bettinger and Bridget Terry Long, "Addressing the Needs of Under-Prepared Students in Higher Education: Does College Remediation Work?" *The Journal of Human Resources* 44, no. 3 (2008): 736–71; Juan Carlos Calcagno and Bridget Terry Long, *The Impact of Postsecondary Remediation Using a Regression Discontinuity Approach: Addressing Endogenous Sorting and Noncompliance* (New York: National Center for Postsecondary Research, 2008).

16. Jaggars and Stacey, *What We Know About Developmental Education Outcomes*.

17. Judith Scott-Clayton, *Do High-Stakes Placement Exams Predict College Success?* (New York: Community College Research Center, Teachers College, Columbia University, 2012); Clive Belfield and Peter M. Crosta, *Predicting Success in College: The Importance of Placement Tests and High School Transcripts* (New York: Community College Research Center, Teachers College, Columbia University, 2012).

18. Bailey, Jeong, and Cho, "Referral, Enrollment, and Completion in Developmental Education Sequences in Community Colleges"; Bettinger and Long, "Addressing the Needs of Under-Prepared Students in Higher Education"; Calcagno and Long, *The Impact of Postsecondary Remediation Using a Regression Discontinuity Approach*.

19. Sara Goldrick-Rab, "Challenges and Opportunities for Improving Community College Student Success," *Review of Education Research* 80, no. 3 (2010): 437–69.

20. Thomas Bailey, Juan Carlos Calcagno, Davis Jenkins, Gregory Kienzl, and Timothy Leinbach, *The Effects of Institutional Factors on the Success of Community College Students* (New York: Community College Research Center, Teachers College, Columbia University, 2005); Juan Carlos Calcagno, Thomas Bailey, Davis Jenkins, Gregory Kienzl, and Timothy Leinbach, "Community College Student Success: What Institutional Characteristics Make a Difference?" *Economics of Education Review* 27 (2008): 632–45.

21. Thomas Bailey, Shanna Smith Jaggars, and Davis Jenkins, *Introduction to the CCRC Assessment of Evidence Series* (New York: Community College Research Center, Teachers College, Columbia University, 2010).

22. Ibid.; John S. Levin, Elizabeth M. Cox, Christine Cerven, and Zachary Haberler, "The Recipe for Promising Practices in Community Colleges," *Community College Review* 38, no. 1 (2010): 31–58; Melinda Mechur Karp, *Toward a New Understanding of Non-Academic Student Support: Four Mechanisms Encouraging Positive Student Outcomes in the Community College*, Assessment of Evidence Series (New York: Community College Research Center, Teachers College, Columbia University, 2011).

23. Linda Serra Hagedorn, "The Pursuit of Student Success: The Directions and Challenges Facing Community Colleges," *Higher Education: Handbook of Theory and Research* 25 (2010): 181–218.

24. Deil-Amen and Rosenbaum, "The Social Prerequisites of Success"; Karp, "Toward a New Understanding of Non-Academic Student Support"; Vince Tinto, *Completing College: Rethinking Institutional Action* (Chicago: University of Chicago Press, 2012); Vince Tinto, *Leaving College: Rethinking the Causes and Cures of Student Attrition*, second edition (Chicago: University of Chicago Press, 1993).

25. Caroline West, Nancy Shulock, and Colleen Moore, *Measuring Institutional Conditions that Support Student Success in the California Community Colleges* (Sacramento, CA: Institute for Higher Education Leadership and Policy, 2012).

26. Center for Community College Student Engagement, *A Matter of Degrees: Practices to Pathways* (Austin, TX: University of Texas at Austin, 2014); Goldrick-Rab, "Challenges and Opportunities for Improving Community College Student Success"; Hagedorn, "The Pursuit of Student Success"; West, Shulock, and Moore, *Measuring Institutional Conditions that Support Student Success in the California Community Colleges*; Bailey, Jaggars, and Jenkins, *Introduction to the CCRC Assessment of Evidence Series*.

27. 21st-Century Commission on the Future of Community Colleges, *Reclaiming the American Dream: Community Colleges and the Nation's Future* (Washington, DC: American Association of Community Colleges, 2012); Byron McClenney and Margaretta Mathis, *Making Good on the Promise of the Open Door: Effective Governance and Leadership to Improve Student Equity, Success, and Completion* (Washington, DC: Association of Community College Trustees, 2011).

28. McClenney and Mathis, *Making Good on the Promise of the Open Door*.

29. The Aspen Institute, *2011 Aspen Prize for Community College Excellence* (Washington, DC: The Aspen Institute, College Excellence Program, 2011); The Aspen Institute, *2013 Aspen Prize for Community College Excellence* (Washington, DC: The Aspen Institute, College Excellence Program, 2013); The Aspen Institute, *2015 Aspen Prize for Community College Excellence* (Washington, DC: The Aspen Institute, College Excellence Program, 2015).

30. The Carnegie Foundation for the Advancement of Teaching, "Strengthening Pre-Collegiate Education in Community Colleges: Project Summary and Recommendations," in *A Report from Strengthening Pre-Collegiate Education in Community Colleges (SPECC)* (Stanford, CA: The Carnegie Foundation for the Advancement of Teaching, 2008).

31. Shanna Smith Jaggars, Nikki Edgecombe, and Georgia W. Stacey, *What We Know About Accelerated Developmental Education* (New York: Columbia University, Teachers College, Community College Research Center, 2014).

32. Center for Community College Student Engagement, *A Matter of Degrees*.

33. Debra D. Bragg, "Examining Pathways to and through the Community College for Youth and Adults," *Higher Education: Handbook of Theory and Research* 26 (2011): 355–93; Goldrick-Rab, "Challenges and Opportunities for Improving Community College Student Success"; Davis Jenkins and Sung Woo Cho, "Get with the Program . . . and Finish It: Building Guided Pathways to Accelerate Student Completion," *New Directions for Community Colleges* 164 (2013): 27–35; West, Shulock, and Moore, *Measuring Institutional Conditions that Support Student Success in the California Community Colleges*.

34. Jenkins and Cho, "Get with the Program . . . and Finish It," 3.

35. Ibid.

36. Thomas R. Bailey, Shanna Smith Jaggars, and Davis Jenkins, *Redesigning America's Community Colleges: A Clearer Path to Student Success* (Cambridge, MA: Harvard University Press, 2015).

37. Center for Community College Student Engagement, *A Matter of Degrees*.

38. Ibid.

39. Ibid.

40. Achieving the Dream, *Intervention Showcase* (Silver Spring, MD: Achieving the Dream), accessed October 1, 2016, http://www.achievingthedream.org/resources/achieving-the-dream-interventions-showcase.

41. Ibid.

42. Center for Community College Student Engagement, *A Matter of Degrees*.

43. Susan Scrivener, Michael J. Weiss, Alyssa Ratledge, Timothy Rudd, Colleen Sommo, and Hannah Fresques, *Doubling Graduation Rates: Three-Year Effects of CUNY's Accelerated Study in Associate Programs (ASAP) for Developmental Education Students* (New York: MDRC, 2015).

44. U.S. Department of Education, *College Completion Toolkit* (Washington, DC: U.S. Department of Education, 2011).

45. National Center for Higher Education Management Systems, *State Policies and Practices Consistent with the National Attainment Agenda* (Boulder, CO: National Center for Higher Education Management Systems, 2014).

46. Martha Snyder, *Driving Better Outcomes: Typology and Principles to Inform Outcomes-Based Funding Models* (Washington, DC: HCM Strategist, 2015).

47. Ibid.

48. Kevin J. Dougherty, Sosanya M. Jones, Hana Lahr, Rebecca S. Natow, Lara Pheatt, and Vikash Reddy, "Looking Inside the Black Box of Performance Funding for Higher Education: Policy Instruments, Organizational Obstacles, and Intended and Unintended Impacts," *The Russell Sage Foundation Journal of the Social Sciences* 2, no. 1 (2016): 147–73.

49. Doug Shapiro, Afet Dundar, Phoebe Khasiala Wakhungu, Xin Yuan, and Autumn T. Harrell, *Transfer and Mobility: A National View of Student Movement in Postsecondary Institutions, Fall 2008 Cohort* (Herndon, VA: National Student Clearinghouse Research Center, 2015).

50. Matthew Smith, *Transfer and Articulation Policies* (Denver, CO: Education Commission of the States, 2015).

51. Davis Jenkins and John Fink, *Tracking Transfer: New Measures of Institutional and State Effectiveness in Helping Community College Students Attain Bachelor's Degrees* (New York: Community College Research Center, Teachers College, Columbia University, 2016).

52. It is important to note that a congressional prohibition prevented the development of a single national student database.

53. Data Quality Campaign, *State Progress* (Washington, DC: Data Quality Campaign), accessed October 1, 2016, http://dataqualitycampaign.org/why-education-data/state-progress/.

54. Institute for Higher Policy, *Envisioning the National Postsecondary Infrastructure in the 21st Century* (Washington, DC: Institute for Higher Education Policy), accessed October 1, 2016, http://www.ihep.org/postsecdata/mapping-data-landscape/national-postsecondary-data-infrastructure.

55. Complete College America, *Time is the Enemy* (Washington, DC: Complete College America, 2011).

56. Ibid.

57. Complete College America, *Four-Year Myth* (Washington, DC: Complete College America, 2014).

58. Doug Shapiro, Afet Dundar, Xin Yuan, Autumn T. Harrell, Justin C. Wild, and Mary B. Ziskin, *Some College, No Degree: A National View of Students with Some College Enrollment, but No Completion* (Herndon, VA: National Student Clearinghouse Research Center, 2014).

59. Clifford Adelman, *Searching for Our Lost Associate's Degrees: Project Win-Win at the Finish Line* (Washington, DC: Institute for Higher Education Policy, 2013).

60. Jason L. Taylor and Debra D. Bragg, *Optimizing Reverse Transfer Policies and Processes: Lessons from Twelve Credit When It's Due States* (Chicago, IL: The Office of Community College Research and Leadership, University of Illinois at Urbana–Champaign, 2015).

FIVE

Pitfalls and Potential of the Completion Agenda

This chapter again draws on interviews conducted with community college presidents in a large Midwest state that has been involved in numerous national completion initiatives. Given their leadership position on campus as well as their role as the lead contact to external stakeholders, their point of view is extremely beneficial.

Whereas chapter 3 examined college presidents' perspectives on the dilemmas facing community colleges, this chapter will explore their views about the completion agenda more specifically. The dilemmas surveyed earlier exist independent of the completion agenda, but each is made more dramatic by the focus on degree completion. This chapter provides a more nuanced reflection by the presidents interviewed about the implications of this decade-long reform agenda.

The discussion that follows is not so much a critique of the focus on degree completion, but instead a measured assessment of the opportunities and challenges this agenda presents. More specifically, this chapter will delve into to the presidents' views on the labor market dynamics that are driving the completion agenda, the implications of increased expectations and accountability that are resulting from this movement, and the role of the primary instigators of much of the reform efforts— foundations and policymakers.

EVOLVING LABOR MARKET REQUIRES A MORE NUANCED APPROACH TO EDUCATIONAL ATTAINMENT

As stated previously, the primary factor driving the completion agenda is global economic competition that in turn has changed the role of and expectations for education. In the first section of the chapter, the views of college presidents about this shift are highlighted. Several presidents who concur with the new economic dynamics suggest that we collectively need a broader view of credentials to meet the labor–market demand for skills. One challenge articulated by a number of those interviewed is a cultural disconnect among some in the general public about the necessity of postsecondary education to garner family-supporting jobs. To remedy this misconception, many of the presidents highlight the need to ensure the programming and credentials offered by their institutions are strongly connected to labor market demand.

Global Competition Is Changing the Role of Education

Most presidents interviewed see the conditions that led to the completion agenda as having resulted from a transformed global economy requiring higher skill levels. They see this change stemming from increased competition for the United States from emerging markets such as China, India, and others. While the United States is still among the leaders in educational attainment globally, our competitive advantage has stagnated as other countries have increased the production of degrees. Comments from presidents echo the sentiment that the relative position of the United States in overall educational attainment has been slipping. The following quote highlights this point:

> What we've seen in the United States for the last 30 years, if not more, is a concern that our students in various levels, K–12 and then in college, might not be keeping up. Our students might not be keeping up with students in other developed countries. There seems to be a body of evidence to support the argument that we're falling behind. It puts more pressure in the last decade upon us, even though the message—the evidence of the message of falling behind has been there for a long time. When people have the economic situation that we've had in the United States, people aren't employed and people see the economy sputtering along and people look around and say, "Hey, things seem to popping in Brazil and things seem to be hopping and popping in China and there's probably an educational component to that."

The forecasts from prominent economists and national reports have substantially influenced the dialogue about postsecondary education and attainment in the United States. The outlook that contributed to these reports now also permeates the decision making of policymakers and philanthropic organizations, as illustrated by the completion initiatives listed in chapter 1.[1] This perspective has also influenced the thinking of many community college presidents. The following quote from a long-serving president reflects a sentiment expressed by several others:

> We are at another one of those revolutionary stages where the portion of the population that needs to be educated has gone up dramatically. The first one was after the Second World War when you had all those G.I.s coming back.

You had a whole generation so we provided great access for those folks at that point. Now with the digital revolution and the transformation of the worldwide economy we have another need to ratchet up. Just look at what's happened with the globalization of our economy. We are in a place where the birth and death of industries and companies and jobs is on an accelerated scale and what does that require from an employee perspective, from a workforce perspective? It requires a lot more education, a lot more training, and a lot more re-training. It's a continuous education process. We've got a rapidly changing economy requiring new skills, new abilities, new knowledge, new content and you have a more rapid churning of employment causing people to have to stay in the educational process. So you've got huge change taking place.

The emerging consensus that more education is required for individuals to be productive in good paying jobs is, for some, seen as vindication of their long-held view of the importance of education. A president from one of the small colleges points out that "I've never had anybody bring me a problem, a societal problem, that education wasn't the solution." As purveyors of education, community college presidents might be expected to take this view. However, the underlying dynamic that is driving the completion agenda is magnifying this simplistic notion. The idea that education is a cure for many societal ills is not new, but the push for postsecondary credentials as an illustration of marketable knowledge and skills is a fairly recent phenomenon—particularly in the community college sector. A president nearing retirement described the trend this way:

If you look at the year 1960, about sixty percent of the jobs in this country could be handled with just a high school education. In this area, with the automotive plants, you could graduate from high school, get a good job, work for 30 or 40 years, and have a great life. About twenty percent of the jobs required something beyond high school and about twenty percent of the jobs required a four-year degree. Now let's jump forward to this decade. The jobs you can get with a high school education are now estimated at about fifteen percent and beyond that about sixty-five percent for what we would call two-year education. Interestingly enough, the baccalaureate is still about twenty to twenty-five percent. That hasn't changed a great deal. With all the emphasis that we have on getting college degrees the number of jobs requiring bachelor's degrees is still only twenty to twenty-five percent. But you can see from those statistics that there is an obvious increased pressure for completion, however you define completion, and that means something beyond high school.

Another president in a rural area expressed a similar sentiment, but he goes further by pointing out the significant challenges those individuals with less education will face in the job market:

It's a reality that 85 percent of the jobs now require an education beyond high school. High school is not the gold standard anymore. That jobs require—any skilled job now requires—an education beyond high school. Just take our state for example, in this area our college completion rate is 15 to 18 percent depending upon which county you're talking about, which lags the state, which is at 30 percent. The state lags the nation, which is about 37 percent. If you look at 85 percent of the jobs require a college education—85 percent of our population are vying for that 15 percent that are unskilled jobs. That's an unsustainable formula and really a formula for disaster if you're trying to build the economy.

Most of the presidents interviewed at one point or another talked about the broader economic conditions that are creating the pressure for higher graduation rates and most, at least rhetorically, are supportive of the completion agenda in general. What is also clear from the conversations with the presidents is that they are thinking about the value proposition of the credentials they offer, perhaps in ways they had not considered or advocated in the past. The next section will explore their nuanced views of certificates and degrees.

A Broader View of Credentials Is Needed

Several presidents voiced concern about an overemphasis on four-year degrees to the exclusion of sub-baccalaureate credentials. A president at one of the smaller rural colleges stated, "My fear is that when we talk so broadly about completion, everyone is still in our society defining that as a four-year degree. We've got to get away from that. That is a mistake." While this may be a true statement, the perception of who goes to college and what a typical college experience looks like is still largely viewed through the lens of a traditional student who goes away to college, lives in a dorm, and completes a bachelor's degree in four years. In fact, as the quote below from one president indicates, he has board members who may not have an appreciation for the value of an associate degree or certificates:

> If a trustee has gone to a private college and done well and now is a profes-
> sional, they assume that that is the path for every community college stu-
> dent. Now, that's going to correct itself as more and more people in leader-
> ship have associate's degrees. We need to realize that [the] associate's degree
> on the education scene is somewhat new within the last 30 years.

A common if not explicit refrain among the presidents is that we col-
lectively need to get away from the notion that the only postsecondary credentials of value are bachelor's degrees or higher. This perception is certainly fed by an idealized, albeit misinformed, view of what a college student is today. There is little question about the correlation between

higher education attainment (that is, BA and above) and higher incomes. However, analysis of the labor market demands reveals the future will require education beyond high school, but not necessarily a bachelor's degree.[2] This is not to say that students should not strive for a baccalaureate or more. Rather, as the quote below from a president at one of the large urban colleges suggests, a broader perspective is needed that recognizes the days of working in one job for an entire career are a thing of the past and frequent retraining and additional education will be critical:

> We need to move past the idea that going to college is an event for very young adults. Say you're 18 to 22 and this is an important part of your life where you're going to go off to college and do all these things . . . it's going to launch you into the world for the next 30, 40 years. That's not the case for [all]—it might be the case for some people—but for other people, you're going to go to college for a while, you're going to get a certificate or let's say you get a degree, but five years later you're going to go back and get a certificate in something. Then three years after that, you're going to take a couple classes. Then ten years after that, you're going to go a whole other direction. I think this continuous retraining is going to be with us for a while.

This quote implicitly references a trend of creating career pathways that connect shorter-term certificates and longer-term degrees in specific fields in ways that are additive for both students and employers.[3] The career pathway concept recognizes that students—particularly at community colleges—enroll for a variety of reasons and the colleges should be sure they leave with a credential that is valuable in the marketplace. Another president reinforces this point by suggesting that "new ideas about credentialing are in order. I think certificates need to be recognized as a valid terminal credential." He also suggests that a more sophisticated data system would allow the field to "define success in ways that are far more individualized."

An enduring issue with sub-baccalaureate education, particularly certificates, is that there is little agreement about what constitutes the curriculum for these short-term credentials.[4] As a result, certificates are difficult to define and track, which in turn makes it difficult to articulate their value or reward the colleges for offering them. One president complains that the state's funding formula doesn't reward them for "moving someone along a workforce completion agenda." She continues by saying that there is no incentive to award certificates because "they don't give us a dime for it." This president clearly sees certificates as an important component of the community college completion agenda, but the challenges of measurement and data collection will likely be an ongoing issue.

In this section the discussion has focused on which credentials should be part of the completion discussion. The presidents interviewed clearly see the need to have a dialogue that emphasizes the importance of associate degrees and certificates as well as bachelor's degrees. The next section will explore what presidents see as a more fundamental challenge facing postsecondary education institutions and the proponents of increased education attainment—a significant portion of the population does not view education beyond high school as critical.

Cultural Dissonance about the Value of Higher Education

One obstacle to boosting completion rates identified by a number of the presidents interviewed relates to a fundamental disconnect between the general public's perceived value of higher education and the human capital demands economists have projected. Historically, a large percentage of the population in industrial Midwest states have not continued their education after graduating from high school because well-paying manufacturing jobs were plentiful and additional schooling was not a prerequisite for these positions. The globally competitive economy has upended this scenario, and as a long-serving president at a large urban college stresses, overcoming the deeply engrained mindset will require a cultural shift:

> I think in the Midwest there is a sense that one has to have higher education, something beyond the secondary, to be successful in the careers of the future. I think the challenge has been convincing the public and changing the culture in our state to understand the benefit of higher education long term for high-wage, high-skill kinds of jobs. That takes time because when you could graduate from high school and get a good job and keep that job the need for higher education just wasn't imbedded in our culture.

The problems posed by the changing economy and the cultural resistance to postsecondary education are made more problematic by demographic shifts projected in the region. Many states in the Midwest have an aging population that will result in a decline in the number of high school graduates over the next decade.[5] This trend does not bode well for the states' economies. If the future workforce is not adequately prepared for the skills demanded by the labor market, employers will look to other geographic areas with a better-skilled workforce. The following quote highlights a similar concern expressed by several presidents:

> We're in a position today where the workforce coming behind is anticipated to be less educated than the current workforce. We're going to have huge challenges in educating the replacement workforce because there are fewer of them coming out of high school with the level of preparation. The percentage of the population with a high school diploma has stagnated in the last 10 years. In fact, it now appears to be diminishing.

The comment below echoes this point, emphasizing that the success of the future workforce will rely upon retraining the current labor force:

> If you look at the demographics, what you see is that in order for this econ-
> omy in five and 10 and 15 years from now to have the workers that it needs,
> we are going to have to bring in people who are already in the workforce
> and retrain them. The baby boom impact, the bubble that's about to burst, is
> going to result in these tremendous vacancies in entire sectors.

Relying on the retraining of the current workforce is problematic for two reasons. First, it is a short-term solution because these individuals will ultimately retire, leading to significant skills gaps. Second, many of the older individuals in this group requiring retraining have enjoyed a comfortable lifestyle to this point without postsecondary education; as one president suggests, they may not be willing or interested in seeking additional training. The undervaluing of education is problematic in indirect ways as well. If adults have less appreciation for education, it is likely the next generation will undervalue it as well. Children who grow up in households without anyone with postsecondary degrees are less likely to go to college, and those that do face considerable barriers as first-generation college students.[6]

For all of these reasons, changing the college-going culture will be an enduring problem. This challenge is further exacerbated over the long term as result of the "brain drain" phenomenon in which a certain percentage of the students who leave to go to college never return to their hometown and those that remain in college will require additional education and training. The president of smaller college highlights this problem:

> This community loses its top 25 percent. We send them off to college and
> they don't come back. That means we have to educate the population we
> have left. If we don't do that, we're not going to survive as a region. I think
> that is imperative that it's not just about teaching the skills necessary. It's
> about changing. It's about a paradigm shift. It's about helping the commu-
> nity understand the importance of education. My warpath in the community
> is to work with the CEOs, and work with the economic development orga-
> nizations, and do all those kinds of things necessary to foster that paradigm
> shift in this community.

Of course, getting additional education or training just for the sake of it does not necessarily translate into gainful employment. In the next section, the views of college presidents highlight that their colleges need to do a better job ensuring the programs offered are well aligned with labor market demand.

Labor Market Value of the Credentials Is Key

"It's all about jobs . . . whether it takes eight years to get a job or a one-year certificate or even a course, it's all about jobs." This quote from a president at a small institution reflects the perspective community college practitioners often share about their students—they enroll to upgrade their skills to get a good paying job.

What is unclear—and much contested among community college advocates—is whether students enroll in these institutions with the intention of getting a credential. Part of the challenge in promoting increased educational attainment from a community college perspective is that credentials have generally not been the message used by the colleges to promote their value. Community colleges have historically sought to meet the needs of their communities by offering short- and longer-term training that may or may not result in a certificate or degree. The shift in emphasis toward credential attainment, as the following president at a mid-size suburban college indicates, is changing the perspective about what the goal of education should be:

> I've seen a shift of public perception of higher education that in general the economy used to be there to support education. Today, education is being viewed as here to support the economy. And I think that is really germane to the discussion of community colleges around workforce development, and I think community colleges are at risk of being viewed strictly as training sites.

While the presidents interviewed say they have always been concerned with the value of their institutions' programmatic offering to employers, several argue that the focus on attainment of credentials changes this dynamic. They express concern about awarding certificate and degree programs that are not aligned with employers' needs. The implication for students, as expressed by this president, is that the credential they earn may be of limited value if it doesn't meet labor market demand:

> The inference is that if we can get more people through our colleges and into degrees that the economy will be better off at the end of the day and that may be true, but it may not always be true. I guess this is my management side coming out in me, but just because someone has a degree doesn't mean they're going to get a job. The jobs also have to be there. People don't want to talk about that in this completion agenda, but it is something that we've got to pay attention to in leadership roles because, again, just getting people through for the purpose of getting them through and saying we were successful . . . well, what were you successful in doing?

Another president at a large urban institution echoed this sentiment, suggesting that colleges need to be thinking about the labor market value of the program students pursue. However, he also signaled that colleges need to balance the students' interest with an educational path that will lead them to gainful employment:

> If you complete a degree in something that you just cannot get a job in, that might be personally fulfilling. On that whole hierarchy of needs it might be very personally fulfilling for you to be able to play and repair ancient musical instruments from antiquity, but you might not be able to get a job in that. It might be personally fulfilling and very much self-actualizing, but you might not be able to put food on the table. We need to make sure that we have balance in that and so that we have people who actually can make a living and then also seek those things in life that give them pleasure. There are things that you complete that don't help you, and you're sitting there unemployed. I think we have a lot of people that are in that boat.

This quote implicitly highlights a key argument in the discussion of the "value" of a college education. As noted previously, community colleges often promote their value in the context of labor market implications and not in terms of personal exploration or enrichment—the hallmark of a more traditional liberal arts education. One of the presidents raised the philosophical question about which people get to have the opportunity to "explore their chosen career," while others are quickly shuffled into a track that may or may not have been adequately considered. This is one of the critiques about the current dialogue about improving outcomes by streamlining and accelerating program pathways and limiting the array of choices students have to make. As the same individual wondered aloud, "what if a student who moves quickly through a welding program discovers after four years that they don't want to be a welder . . . have we done this person a disservice because we rushed them through a program?"

While this tension between the labor market implications of a postsecondary education and a student's opportunity to explore their interests is not new, one president suggests that the ultimate measure is that "people have a credential that will enable them to improve their lives. That is the bigger picture." Attaining one credential does not guarantee that a student will not have to return to school to further enhance their skills. In fact, this quote argues that job requirements in a specific field evolve over time and colleges and students need to stay in tune with these changes to ensure the continued marketability of their skill sets:

> I've watched, for example, the physician assistant program, which is a very strong program for some colleges, and over the years now, physician assistants moved to requiring a baccalaureate degree. Then it moved to requiring a master's degree. Now it's moving to the doctorate level. There are any numbers of programs that we've all had, where at one point in time the as-

sociate degree was enough, but you're seeing an escalation. For others the associate's degree is enough, and you haven't seen that same escalation.

There is an overarching theme through the interviews that labor market demand is not static and will evolve over time. On some level this has always been true, but the globalization of the economy and the corresponding demand for higher levels of credentials are forcing colleges to think differently about their students and the programs they offer. A president from a large urban college suggested that the recent economic crisis has greatly influenced the dialogue about aligning skill and credential attainment with labor market demand:

> In the years since the great recession there's this general idea that we need people with the right skills to help improve our economy, so we have more productive people who are able to compete in a global economy. I think we're already getting back to [skill] shortages again.

As the presidents talk about labor market demand for their colleges' programs, the recent recession and ensuing slow recovery have made it difficult for them to parse the short-term economic downturn from longer-term structural changes in the economy. This issue is also playing out for graduates from the colleges. One president was rather emotional on this point: "I'm really worried about the economy because we are getting graduates who are not finding jobs." She continues, saying, "I don't want to be a part of a school that has a mission that isn't true."

On one level, this comment reflects the reality of a slow economic recovery. In another sense this quote suggests a misalignment between increasing expectations about student outcomes from programs that are not in demand by employers. Presidents argued in several instances that if there isn't a collective effort to ensure the credential students earn has labor market value, the desired effect for students, the local communities, and the state will not be realized. This line of thinking suggests that accountability systems that are put in place, which will be discussed in more detail in the next section, need to focus on credential attainment *and* labor market demand.

INCREASED ACCOUNTABILITY AND EXPECTATIONS MAY CREATE UNINTENDED CONSEQUENCES

The fiscal crisis of the past several years has led to significant constraints on public resources. This has created an environment in which policymakers—reflecting public sentiment—are asking more questions about what they are getting for the tax dollars being allocated. This heightened level of accountability is not aimed solely at postsecondary institutions. However, when fiscal constraints are paired with the demand for increased educational attainment, the rationale for the college completion agenda becomes intense. One of the presidents described the situation well in this quote:

> I think that there's a conspiracy. I think what's driving it [the completion agenda] to a great degree from the federal government is the fact that a group of influential people have realized how much money the federal government is spending. They want more accountability for the dollars that they're spending. The same thing is true on the state level. It's even worse on the state level because most states have experienced significant shortfalls. They're looking for ways to cut back on all spending, including higher education. It's easy to pick out the sectors that have the highest funding amounts and say, there's got to be more accountability there. I also think that higher education has flaunted itself to the general public.

In general, the presidents were accepting of the increased scrutiny that comes with stronger accountability, with a president of a smaller institution stating directly, "We are being held to be accountable, accountable for our resources, and accountable for the success of our students. I see that as a good thing." Some believe, as the previous quote insinuates, that higher education institutions have not been as accountable as they should. One of the newer presidents suggests that community colleges should not be surprised by the focus on completion given the track record on graduation rates:

> If the completion rate is 20 or 21 percent that just doesn't look good. If people just look at that and they don't think too deeply about it, that just doesn't look good, so if I am a legislator and I am starting to hear—especially in the political environment with the funding discussions and how much money that the government pours into higher education—and look [at] what we get, that is why it's [the completion agenda] no doubt part of the conversation. When you get somebody like Bill Gates paying attention to it and saying why can't we do better with this and willing to back it up substantially—that is why it's getting attention.

A common concern in the conversations with presidents about increases in accountability and expectations is the greater focus on the return on the public investments in colleges. This marks a departure from the historical view of higher education, according to a long-serving president who is nearing retirement. He says he sees "pressures to run our colleges more as a business today." He continues suggesting that some expectation around efficiency, effectiveness, and outcomes is warranted, but "the emphasis has shifted away from what we're doing for people to more of how we are running the college as a business."

This shift in emphasis is indicative of broader societal shifts toward a market orientation that values efficiency over other attributes. It is a mindset reinforced in the rhetoric of other presidents. For example, when describing policymaker perspectives about higher education expenditures and outcomes, another president stated that "the federal government and state governments are tired of pouring money—vast amounts of money—into systems that produce 16 percent success. As a businessman, none of us would tolerate that. As a nation we shouldn't tolerate it either." Putting a finer point on the emerging consensus about degree attainment, a president of one of the largest colleges channels the perceived view of policymakers about the completion agenda in the following quote:

> I think states are going to say, "we're not willing to pay for somebody who wants to come that are just there for enrichment and improvement because the dollars we're putting into education will be for productive citizens who are going to work and add to the economy." That state or national investment in higher education will be for people who say "I want a degree. My goal is a degree. The courses that I take will lead me to a degree, not just for some college."

While most of the presidents didn't predict how some of these conversations on accountability would play out, they generally viewed the trend toward higher expectations and greater scrutiny as something that would not recede with time. Echoing the self-critique of community colleges offered by one of the presidents, another referred to accountability as a "sticky wicket" that was here to stay and suggested that while it is being driven by external forces, colleges have themselves to blame because "we brag about our successes and ignore our failures . . . and our failures are legion." This comment reflects the view held by a number of presidents, who also said they need to tackle the challenges they face head on or someone (that is, policymakers) would do it for them through more prescriptive mandates. The same president also said, "demonstrating that we're actually doing what we say we're doing is much easier said than done."

Potential Impacts of Outcomes-Based Funding

The presidents interviewed expressed a variety of concerns about accountability standards in general and the implications of performance funding specifically. The worries shared included the impact on their colleges individually and collectively, but some presidents raised the prospect that students would be negatively impacted as well:

> What I'm afraid of is that we'll start becoming primarily numbers driven. The students may wind up being the ones who lose in the long run, especially

the ones that need a lot of help, because the focus will be on retention and completion. The ones that are not strong enough or capable enough could very well fall by the wayside. We could put all our emphasis on resources and efforts on the ones that are going to complete so we can maximize our state funding. That scares me. I hope this door never closes. I've said this to my staff, I'm afraid that the open door is starting to close.

This quote was one of the more pointed arguments about the negative impact of the completion agenda, and it suggests that colleges could begin to make choices in reaction to funding realities that will cause the least prepared students to suffer as a result.

Another bothersome possibility expressed in several interviews was that colleges might also find creative ways to essentially game the new funding formulas to their benefit. This may entail focusing on students who are more likely to succeed, as the previous comment suggests. It might also lead to an equally problematic trend of colleges lowering standards and expectation to ensure a larger percentage of students reach the various momentum points the formula rewards. A president at a large college suggested that attention should be paid to the possibility that colleges will behave in ways that are contrary to the intent of new funding formulas:

I think we need to be vigilant and on guard for unintended consequences. There's always the possibility of unintended consequences. The most egregious possibility—and I don't think what I'm about to say will necessarily come true—but the most egregious unintended consequence would be colleges watering down their standards and passing students through just so that they can make their numbers look better. The question is how to provide safeguards against that.

Beyond manipulating the system, a few presidents raised the issue that colleges have very different ways of doing things and this may impact their position in funding formulas compared to other institutions. For example, depending on an individual college's approach assessing and placing students into developmental education courses, the institution may be advantaged or disadvantaged not because of the actual success of their students, but because of the practices and policies they have in place.

The issue of how one college performs under an outcomes-based funding formula in relation to other institutions was a prominent theme in the interviews. Because of the way funding might be distributed through a defined pot of money, colleges essentially compete against each other for the funds. As one president indicates, colleges that "figure out a way to have their students complete more course work and complete more certificate degrees and transfer at higher rate than other colleges, they will get a greater share of money."

Without knowing the exact dollar figures, it was relatively easy to discern those institutions that were doing well under the formula and those that were not based on the presidents' comments. Presidents of those colleges fairing more poorly tended to object to the competition the formula created between institutions. One president from a large urban college said his primary concern is that "in order for any college to gain resources it's got to be at the expense of other colleges." He continues by questioning the sustainability of a funding model under which a college "can grow and still lose money."

The opposing view from a president whose institution has fared better takes the long view, suggesting that implementing policies that can help the college benefit from the components of the formula is essential. He calls out his peers, stating that "they're not performing as well as others" and that they all agreed to the formula so "why should it be changed now?" It is difficult to predict the longevity of current funding formulas, but if the frustration exhibited in the following quote becomes more pervasive among the presidents, modifications seem likely:

> Gore Vidal once said, it is not enough that I succeed. My friends must also fail. When you look at the funding formula, you can have growth. If you're not growing quite as fast as your sister institutions, you'll get less money this year than last. It really is like that. We live in a system where we wish for failure of everyone else except us. That's a hell of a formula.

Acknowledging the competition for limited resources under the new formula, several presidents also raised the paradox that stronger accountability and performance funding models may have very little impact on what happens in the classroom. A newer president stated it this way:

> I will tell you where all that stuff breaks down. It breaks down at the classroom level because there is not a faculty member that is going to be held accountable. What is the closest source of success? It is whether or not the student is learning that which we have decided is important for them to learn. If I am a professor and my view is my job is to teach them, alright, my job is to provide the material, but I don't view it as my responsibility to make sure that they learn it or to be available during office hours, on and on and on.

While this quote represents a longstanding excuse for why students' outcomes have been so stubbornly low, it is also reflective of an organizational reality that presidents must balance as they attempt to steer their colleges in a different direction.

A president nearing retirement repeats the challenge of impacting what happens in the classroom, but he does not place all the blame on faculty alone. Instead he points out that "part of it is faculty resistance.

Part of it is institutional ignorance and institutional will." There is no question that faculty legitimately see the curriculum as their purview, but as another president pointed out, there is a tendency to use academic freedom as a scapegoat for avoiding the work of building constructive dialogue. Asked about the prospects of engaging faculty in the conversation about the completion agenda, a long-serving president shared the following perspective:

> I think that's where the challenge is. I'm not saying that any of this is impossible, nor is it necessarily unrealistic. I think in the kind of society we have today, there's got to be accountability. No question about it. But how do you turn this gigantic ship around in the middle of this ocean? You're not going to change faculty attitudes overnight.

However, one president from a rural college argues that those promoting increased accountability can't lose sight of the individualized nature of education and how choices students make also impact the outcome:

> I think that as long as we're being held to these standards, we have to appreciate the fact that at the heart of our industry are highly individualized human beings who are and can be terribly fickle. It would be a dreadful crime to ever get to a point where we're being penalized for not being able to fit multi-dimensional people into very square categories. I think that would be a really sad thing. I'm a bit afraid of the funding formula. I'm a bit afraid because if in fact we find ourselves financially penalized for not meeting goals that are too rigid or too stringent in their technical definitions, it's not going to help anything. I want to be inspired by the challenge that the formula presents. I want to be inspired to think that excellence will be rewarded.

This section explored how presidents described broad shifts in terms of both globalization of the economy and increased accountability for public resources. The challenges created for community colleges are considerable, and the shift in expectations discussed here has precipitated competing logics of access versus completion in the field. The final section of this chapter will examine college presidents' perspectives of the role of foundations and policymakers in promoting change in community colleges.

FOUNDATIONS AND POLICYMAKERS: AGENTS FOR CHANGE OR MICROMANAGERS?

In the discussion with the presidents about shifting dynamics resulting in increased accountability, there was also dialogue about where the pressures being exerted on community colleges were coming from more

specifically. In most interviews this discussion centered on state and federal policymakers as well as major foundations funding reform efforts
nationally. There is no doubt from the interviews with presidents that
the external pressure exerted by these two broad groups of actors created political conditions ripe for the completion agenda to emerge. The
next two subsections examine the presidents' views on foundations and
policymakers, respectively.

Influence of Foundations on the Completion Agenda

As discussed in chapter 1, several national foundations have played a substantial role in promoting the completion agenda. The Bill and Melinda
Gates Foundation, Lumina Foundation for Education, Ford Foundation,
Kresge Foundation, and others sponsored a variety of initiatives that are
promoting the adoption of policies and practices that will help them realize their ambitious completion goals. By mobilizing multiple constituents
within the field, such as presidents, trustees, associations, policymakers,
and the research community, foundations have sought to influence the
behavior of colleges from a variety of perspectives. One of the individuals interviewed made the distinction between the role of large national
funders and local community or regional foundations: "there are only a
few foundations that have enough resources that they can set an agenda
and drive systemic change." It is these foundations that have played a
prominent role in promoting the completion agenda.

Two overarching themes emerged from the interviews with presidents about philanthropic organizations. The first was that foundation
resources serve as catalysts to help college leadership transform their colleges. The second theme was actually a concern about the sustainability
and scalability of work occurring under the guise of these grant-funded
initiatives. Interestingly, presidents' views toward the actions of foundations were generally more favorable than those of state and federal policymakers. This positive view was prevalent despite the fact that foundations have also pursued aggressive strategies at the state and local levels
to influence completion-related policies (that is, performance funding,
alignment between educational sectors).

Presidents overall have a supportive view of the investments foundations have made to improve student success in the community college
sector. Many see the funding and attention as critical for raising awareness about the challenges colleges face, creating synergies and models
for reform, and, perhaps most importantly, filling gaps in resources. One
president described the efforts of the foundations in the context of the
work of two of the larger completion initiatives underway:

All of the challenges that you see with Achieving the Dream and Completion by Design are going to be with us for a long time. This is a big issue. This is important work that we're doing because somehow we've got to transform our delivery systems to better engage and nurture those disparate learners to get them to a credential.

The notion of transformational change at colleges is difficult to achieve without external pressure and support. The major national foundations have been critical of community colleges, but they have also offered possible solutions. As the work of the completion agenda has matured over the past ten years, the foundations have developed stronger points of view about the innovations that seem to be working. In this respect, new funding is increasingly tied to specific modes or approaches. The following quote by a president at a small college suggests that this testing of intervention models is vital:

Gates [Foundation] and some other groups are beginning to say, "look traditional approaches aren't working. We need new approaches." They're putting pressures on us to get people through degree programs . . . to be successful. They've developed these models to say "here's a way to do it."

To continue with this point, some have argued that the models promoted by foundations are too prescriptive and have not been adequately tested. However, one president responded to criticisms of the foundations' approach by saying they are "going to have an agenda, but they're not forcing anybody to take their money, so it's still up to the individual college to decide if the Gates [Foundation] agenda fits the college's agenda."

There were subtle references to the efficacy of some of the things foundations were promoting. For example, a president from one of the larger colleges that has been involved in a number of the national initiatives made the following statement:

The philanthropic organizations are doing the right kinds of things. They're trying to provide resources; they're trying to use their resources and their power to make good things happen. So I think they're generally well intended. I think we're early in that process to undergo and understand to what degree they've been successful, but, again, I appreciate the fact that they're focused on the things that matter to us.

This president is clearly supportive of the work of the foundations, but he also notes the relative newness of these efforts, suggesting we need to be patient enough to see what the impact will be. This sentiment about patience was also a point made by another interviewee as a weakness of relying on foundations to drive the completion agenda. More specifically, this person noted that the major foundations have "short attention spans" and they often are not willing to let the process of innovation play out.

Continuing with the theme of the sustainability of foundation support for efforts to support the completion agenda, a president—whose college has not been involved in many of the initiatives—raises the question of how colleges keep the work going without grant funds:

> They're well intentioned—whether it is Gates [Foundation] or another foundation—I mean their heart is in the right place. They want to create systemic change; whether they will or not I think remains to be seen. When the funding is pulled, what will remain—I couldn't really tell you, but I think they are well intended. It is just like any grant funding or even Achieving the Dream and I am no expert on that, but each of the colleges kind of did their own thing—some obviously more successful than others.

This quote alludes to the consistency with which new interventions or strategies are applied across colleges to improve student outcomes. This point, which will be discussed in more detail in the next chapter, was also raised in a 2011 evaluation report of the first five years of work under the Achieving the Dream initiative, in which evaluators noted that there had been too much variation in the type of interventions piloted by colleges to really gauge the effectiveness of the initiative overall.[7]

Several comments from presidents reflected this issue of scalability of interventions piloted through their foundation-supported work as a key barrier to really moving completion numbers. In discussing the overall value of the foundations' role, one president said the issue for them is "how do we translate that [intervention] from a group of 25 students to 1,000 students—to the masses—taking it to scale? That's our challenge. How are we going to take this Gates model to scale?" This comment comes from a large college in which the challenge appears to be designing interventions that can actually be expanded to a larger number of their students with adequate support in place. A president from a smaller college highlights a different dynamic:

> There's a lot of emphasis on scaling up [interventions that work]. It's much more difficult to scale up at a small college than it is a large college. At a large college, you do something and it works, and then you expand it to a greater population. Now you're affecting a good portion of students. At a small college, we can proportionally have the same effect or even a greater effect within our institution, but how much that contributing to the overall goal is less impactful. The way we have to scale up is export best practices to other colleges that can use what we've done and take it to a larger population. I've been emphasizing that really the small colleges need to network in

order to have that kind of impact. If we do network, we'll have just as much an impact as the larger colleges do, but it's a different approach.

The issue of scale from this president's perspective is that small colleges, because of the costs involved, can only reach so many students regardless of how well an intervention is designed. Several of the recent student success or completion initiatives, like Completion by Design, have tried to remedy this issue from the start by designing the interventions with scaling to large numbers of students.

Overall the presidents view the major foundations playing an important role in raising awareness about the completion agenda and community colleges more generally. As one president indicated, "it's no accident that the profile of community colleges increased when the Lumina and Gates [Foundations] got interested. Having community colleges more prominently placed in the psyche of the public is nothing but positive." The general view is that the foundations have also served as a catalyst for promoting organizational change and reform. In a telling comment about the value of the foundations' focus on completion and innovation, one president suggested that it wasn't the financial support resources as much as the impetus for change that foundations provided through the prominent national initiatives:

> We have been fortunate to leverage some of those resources from Gates [Foundation], Achieving the Dream, and others. We have one college in the state that went through Achieving the Dream on their own dime, and there are other schools that are doing that right now. Looking back on it, if I had to do it, I would have done it because it really transformed this institution.

The next section examines the presidents' views of policymakers and their role in promoting the completion agenda at the state and federal level. As noted previously, the presidents' tone about policymakers was markedly different and more negative compared to foundations.

Appropriate Role of Policymakers

> The role of government in education is to ensure that from a citizenry standpoint, the citizen has the opportunity. That's not to say they will or will not take advantage of it, but the citizen has the chance to advance, to have choices, and to have opportunities.

This quote from a president at a suburban college reflects the general recognition among those interviewed of the appropriate function of government in supporting educational opportunities. There were two predominant themes that emerged in the interviews about the role of policymakers, both of which reflected a need for balance. The first theme speaks to the desire for a balance between consistent yet flexible policies in place. This theme is also reflective of some of the discussion earlier about the use of performance funding to incentivize changes in college behavior. The second theme focused on policymakers as regulators versus facilitators of change. Several presidents noted that at times the roles that policymakers play are at cross purposes. It is important to note that the presidents' comments about policymakers, unlike those about foundations, tended to reflect a broader perspective on issues such as governance and institutional autonomy rather than a more narrow focus on degree completion.

As leaders of their colleges, the presidents generally favor autonomy and flexibility to guide their institutions based on the needs of the communities they serve. The notion that state or federal policymakers can dictate what they can and cannot do on their individual campuses is not well received by most. One president made the following statement when talking about the increasing pressure coming from the state:

> Mandating what we should do and how we should do it is overly intrusive. I think it really could lead to a one size fits all type of philosophy. I think that's what many of us are fearful of, that kind of intrusion.

Continuing with the theme of an overly intrusive approach from the state, another president expressed concern about the impact of state legislative term limits and the short-term view many elected officials have on thoughtful policy:

> So you've got legislators who quite often have very little tenure in their positions and the institutional knowledge isn't there. At best some of their staffers may have it. So as a result, I think that the election cycles and the impact of the election cycles have really forced a much more short-term vision of the role of not only higher education, but education in general and state public policy even more generally. I think then that you get things like a shifting emphasis in funding trying to impact institutional behavior, resulting in all sorts of unintended consequences that I'm not sure we've fully fleshed out.

As this quote suggests, legislative turnover leads to significant shifts in policy and funding priorities that make it difficult for the colleges to react to local and state needs or demands. Given the increasing important of higher education to the economy, colleges are receiving more attention from the executive branch as well, and recent shifts in the partisan control of the governor's office are also resulting in inconsistent priorities. These changes in administrative and legislative positions have a direct impact on the policy priorities that buffet the colleges with shifting expectations. One president highlights state policy on transfer and articulation as an example of this trend:

Three or four years ago, we were all very concerned about transfer. Transfer is very important, so please don't misunderstand. As that moved into the front seat, what moved into the back seat? Now I think we're seeing a reverse in that. Although transfer will continue to be important, what are we doing for business and industry, entrepreneurship, economic development, and how are we getting workers retrained to reenter the workforce, is equally important. It's hard to serve two masters. That becomes part of the dilemma. It's a balancing act.

While the policy shifts have presented challenges for how colleges should react, they can also have negative implications for students. For example, one of the long-serving presidents discussed how the state political leadership, in an attempt to maximize the base funding available to colleges in the recent economic downturn, changed the way state financial aid was awarded:

The state required federal financial aid to be applied before the state aid and when they did that, what it did was eliminate community college students from being eligible for state financial aid. We used to package state aid first because it could only be used to pay for tuition, whereas the Pell grant could pay for lots of other support for students. What they did was inadvertent, from a policy perspective, but it made our job more difficult because they reduced the full package of support.

The effect of this policy change was to reduce the cost of the financial aid program for the state and, in turn, free up dollars that went to colleges in the form of overall state subsidy, but it had an adverse impact on community college students. The same president continued drawing the connection between cost of attendance and completion rates, stating that "we know that there's an association between enrolling full-time and completion, but we also know that 60 percent of our students are part-time because life is in the way." These students simply can't afford to attend full-time and, as a result of the recent change to state aid policy, they are less likely to do so in the future.

With the recent changes in state financial aid as an example, several presidents note the lack of coherence to the state's approach to higher education policy in general and student progression and completion specifically. One president, comparing his experience in other states, indicated that "this state is all over the place as the community college 'system' has no cohesion in advancing these [completion] issues, no cohesion in helping the colleges refine their missions." This notion of greater consistency stemming from the state's ten-year previous strategic plan for higher education, while welcomed by many presidents, creates the potential for greater state intrusion, as the following comment suggests:

> A lot of what's built in the strategic plan was what has been put forth in other states in terms of tighter collaboration and those kinds of things. I think there's a place for the state to, if nothing else, facilitate collaboration. There's a balance between how much you facilitate and how much mandate.

This quote reflects the sentiment discussed previously that too much state intervention is unhealthy and would diminish the autonomy of the individual campuses. While this view was prevalent in many interviews, some of the presidents voiced a subtle plea to see the state take on a more assertive leadership role. One president, who had only been in the state for a short time, and came from a state with a much stronger governing board, advocated for the state to provide more assertive leadership:

> I think state systems fail to lead from the front when they could, and fail to step to the back when they should. I see it happen a lot. I'm not talking about personalities. I think it's just the way they think. They tend to be afraid of their own power. They tend to deal it out very sparingly. There were so many times when senior leadership at the state could have simply said, "this is the direction we're going." Instead, for every question, there was a system task force. It was all this decision by committee. That's what I mean by leading from the back. There were so many times when I'd say, if they'd only embraced the edict, edicts aren't always a bad thing. Just tell us what you want; you know what I'm saying? So many times I wished the system office could just step forward and say, "you know what, we're going to save you all a lot of time. Let's just do this."

This was an interesting sidebar from what the majority of the presidents wanted, which is less state intervention. From the perspective of policymakers, they often feel institutions are not sufficiently responsive to their demands and, as a result, they adopt policies that may be overly prescriptive and have unintended consequence but push the colleges to alter their behavior. In talking about the role of policymakers in the completion agenda, one president said, "state policy is a blunt tool." However, he continued, "There are very few levers such as funding policymakers can pull to push for change at the institutional level."

To summarize, this chapter explored presidents' perspectives about the factors that have contributed to the emergence of the completion agenda. The presidents voiced concerns that the emphasis on attainment could result in a focus on increasing the raw number of degrees, rather than on the value of the credentials in the labor market. They also noted that sub-baccalaureate certificates and degrees, which their institutions offer, are not receiving enough attention as an important part of the conversation relative to bachelor's degrees. More generally, they see a cultural disconnect about the value of education beyond high school as one of the major obstacles to reaching educational attainment goals.

A second key observation from the presidents interviewed is the trend toward increased accountability for student outcomes. The presidents noted that historically they have been judged largely based on inputs (that is, enrollments). The shift toward a market orientation, which values efficiency, has contributed to the notion that colleges (and all public organizations) need to demonstrate a return on the investment of taxpayer dollars. Presidents noted that this trend, which has been magnified by considerable fiscal constraints in the past decade, has resulted in much more aggressive performance funding formulas that reward colleges for student progression and completion.

Presidents voiced concerns about the unintended consequences of new funding models, including increased competition between colleges, the possibility of colleges manipulating the system, or a trend toward watered down standards to increase completions. They also noted the formula could have a negative impact on the access mission of colleges and actually incentivize them to enroll students who are more likely to finish.

NOTES

1. Cassie Hall and Scott L. Thomas, "'Advocacy Philanthropy' and the Public Policy Agenda: The Role of Modern Foundations in American Higher Education," 93rd Annual Meeting of the American Educational Research Association, Vancouver, Canada, 2012; Alene Russell, *A Guide to Major U.S. College Completion Initiatives* (Washington, DC: American Association of State Colleges and Universities, 2010).

2. Anthony P. Carnevale, "Confessions of an Education Fundamentalist: Why Grade 12 Is Not the Right End Point for Anyone," in *Minding the Gap: Why Intergrating High School with College Makes Sense and How to Do It*, ed. Nancy Hoffman, Joel Vargas, Andrea Venezia, and Marc S. Miller (Cambridge, MA: Harvard Education Press, 2007), 15–26; Anthony P. Carnevale, Nicole Smith, and Jeff Stohl, *Help Wanted: Projections of Jobs and Education Requirements through 2018* (Washington DC: Georgetown University, Center on Education and the Workforce, 2010); National Commission on Community Colleges, *Winning the Skills Race and Strengthening America's Middle Class: An Action Agenda for Community Colleges* (New York: The National Commission on Community Colleges, 2008).

3. W. Norton Grubb, Norena Badway, and Denise Bell, "Community Colleges and the Equity Agenda: The Potential of Noncredit Education," *Annals of the American Academy of Political and Social Science* 586 (2003): 218–40; Barbara K. Townsend, "Blurring the Lines: Transforming Terminal Education to Transfer Education," *New Directions for Community Colleges* 115 (2001): 63–72; Michelle Van Noy and James Jacobs, "The Outlook for Noncredit Workforce Education," *New Directions for Community Colleges* 146 (2009): 87–94.

4. Brian Bosworth, *Certificates Count: An Analysis of Sub-Baccalaureate Certificates* (Washington, DC: Complete College America, 2010); Carnevale, Smith, and Stohl, *Help Wanted*.

5. Patrick Kelly and Julie Strawn, *Not Just Kid Stuff Anymore: The Economic Imperative for More Adults to Complete College* (Washington DC: Center for Law and Social Policy, 2011).

6. Clifford Adelman, *Moving into Town—and Moving on: The Community College in the Lives of Traditional-Age Students* (Washington, DC: U.S. Department of Education, 2005); Gary Hoachlander and C. Dennis Carroll, *Community College Students: Goals, Academic Preparation, and Outcomes* (Washington, DC: National Center for Education Statistics, 2003); Jason E. Lane, "Studying Community Colleges and Their Students: Context and Research Issues," *New Directions for Institutional Research* 118 (2003): 51–67.

7. Elizabeth Zachry Rutschow, Lashawn Richburg-Hayes, Thomas Brock, Genevieve Orr, Oscar Cerna, Dan Cullinan, Monica Reid Kerrigan, Davis Jenkins, Susan Gooden, and Kasey Martin, *Turning the Tide: Five Years of Achieving the Dream in Community Colleges* (New York: MDRC and Community College Research Center, 2011).

Six

Forging a Path to a Sustained Completion Agenda

Public policy can be a useful tool for creating conditions and incentives for innovation. Policies, however, cannot be adopted in a vacuum. Informed policy must include open dialogue with key voices to have impact and staying power. In a similar vein, a reform movement (in any industry) can be difficult to implement and sustain without broad support from stakeholders. Innovation and institutional change require leadership and commitment to move forward. This is true of reform efforts in general and the completion agenda specifically. This chapter explores important questions related to the completion agenda that policymakers and practitioners should consider. Among them are three questions: What has been collectively accomplished in the past decade? What are the obstacles to broad-scale impact? What is needed to promote scaled adoption *and* adaptation of promising practices in the field?

TAKING STOCK OF THE PROGRESS
TOWARD COMPLETION GOALS

Following ten years of calls by state and national policymakers for increased educational attainment, efforts by institutions to improve student outcomes, and investment of hundreds of millions of dollars by foundations, the completion agenda has become a ubiquitous movement that has eclipsed access and equal opportunity as the guiding yardstick for higher education in the United States.

According to a recent survey by the National Center for Higher Education Management Systems, thirty-six states have set (or are in the process of setting) educational attainment goals and an equal number of states have adopted (or are considering) funding formulas that emphasize student outcomes in addition to enrollment. Colleges and universities across the country participate in a patchwork of initiatives that focus on everything from accelerating developmental education and providing greater access to public benefits (beyond traditional financial aid) to efforts that better define student learning outcomes and establish competency-based delivery models.[1] After a decade, it is important to pause and ask: What has been the impact of this activity?

In 2008 the Lumina Foundation published the first edition of *A Stronger Nation through Higher Education*. This report was designed to highlight the gap between where the country stood in terms of education attainment—defined as adults age twenty-five to sixty-four with an associate degree or higher—and Lumina's "Big Goal" of 60 percent of the twenty-five to sixty-four population having a quality postsecondary credential by 2025. In the year this report was published the attainment rate stood at 37.9 percent. Eight years later, the percentage was up to 40.4 percent. Looking more closely at these numbers, the 2016 Lumina report illustrates that there has been a promising increase, albeit modest, in educational attainment across all racial subgroups. Although this is a promising trend, in the years since their first report (and substantial investment) the overall attainment rate has only increased 2.5 percentage points.[2]

Another way to look at our collective progress toward increasing educational attainment levels is to revisit the attainment goal President Obama set in 2009, calling for 60 percent of adults age twenty-five to sixty-four to hold an associate degree or higher by 2020. According to an analysis by the *Chronicle of Higher Education* in January 2015, only 3.7 percent more of the target population reached this attainment level six years after the president set the national goal. With six years until the 2020 target date, a 14.4 percentage point increase will be required to reach the president's goal. Some critics have argued that this goal was too ambitious from the start. Proponents of the completion agenda—and the president's goal—defend the progress to date and suggest that we are only just starting to see the impact of reform efforts.[3]

A third way to gauge progress of the completion agenda is to look at how community colleges measure their progress. A primary recommendation of the American Association of Community Colleges's 21st-Century Commission on the Future of Community Colleges was a call for a 50 percent increase in the rate of completion (certificates and associate degrees) by 2020. This recommendation echoed a commitment by several key organizations—the American Association of Community Colleges, the Association of Community College Trustees, the National Institute for Staff and Organizational Development, the League for Innovation in the Community College, Phi Kappa Theta, and the Center for Community College Student Engagement—to the same goal.[4]

In April 2015 AACC released a progress report on the 50 percent increase by 2020 goal. Using 2009 as a baseline for calculating the number of completions needed by 2020, AACC determined that an additional 4.6

million certificates or degrees would need to be awarded between 2009 and 2020 (above the normal projections) to realize the 50 percent increase. Tracking the progress after four years (through the 2013–14 academic year), AACC found that colleges nationally had awarded 17 percent of the number needed to reach the 2020 goal.[5] This increase represents improvement, but similar to the modest increases measured by the Obama administration and the Lumina Foundation, the progress is coming too slow to reach the 2020 goal. The crucial question is: Why, despite all of the activity and investment over the past decade, have we only modestly moved the needle on attainment and completion rates?

OBSTACLES TO IMPACT

Some rightly point to the fact that a large percentage of community college students come from underrepresented low-income, minority, and first-generation populations that have historically had a postsecondary education gap compared to their better situated peers. Others point to the substantial influx of students into community colleges in the past decade—many of them returning adults—who were negatively impacted by the Great Recession.

Some argue that a large number of students in this group indicate plans to pursue degrees when in fact they enroll for a few courses or short-term certificates to upgrade skills. There is no question that a segment of the community college student population does fall into this "skill builder" category, and research suggests that this group does experience a bump in wages as a result of the skills they attain. It is also true that financial aid policies and practices incentivize a portion of students to misrepresent degree intentions in order to access federal financial aid. However, it is unreasonable to imply that this student population represents a majority of students who enroll at community colleges and stop out short of earning a credential.

Even when we account for dynamics that are largely beyond the control of the institutions, a decade of reform efforts in community colleges has yielded only modest improvement in student outcomes. What are the impediments to completion? Research conducted by Achieving the Dream (ATD), MDRC, and the Community College Research Center (CCRC) reveals challenges standing in the way of completion. ATD has been a prime mover of the completion initiative in community colleges over the past decade. Many partners working with ATD have provided financial resources and technical assistance to nearly two hundred colleges across the country since 2004. The ATD emphasis on institution-wide reform calling for enhanced data capacity to inform college decisions and change organizational culture has had a profound, if difficult to quantify, influence on the completion movement. However, the impact of the work of individual colleges has yet to yield outcomes on the level anticipated at the outset of the initiative.[6]

In the evaluation of the first twenty-six colleges involved in ATD, MDRC and CCRC noted that there had been too much variation in the type of interventions piloted by colleges to gauge overall effectiveness of the completion initiative. While acknowledging funders, partners, and colleges involved in ATD for enhancing dialogue in the field and elevating the conversation of student success, the report went on to indicate that much of the college-level work focused on too few students to move the needle in terms of the population of community college students.

Acknowledging the important contribution ATD has made in promoting the use of data by colleges, the evaluation also noted that much of the emphasis at individual institutions was on the front end of the student experience—particularly for students enrolled in remedial courses—without sufficient attention to students moving on to college-level courses. To be fair, the focus on developmental education was identified as a substantial barrier to completion and clearly warranted attention, but unfortunately this focus has had the effect of limiting the faculty engaged in the dialogue to those teaching developmental or gateway English and mathematics courses.[7]

It is easy in hindsight to look back at a decade of work by ATD and draw critical conclusions about what could have been done differently. While the initiative has had its shortcomings, ATD has served as a clarion call for reform that continues to this day. Despite the slow improvement across all institutions, there has been notable improvement at individual ATD colleges that serves as a valuable example for colleges to emulate. To this end, ATD created the designation "Leader College" to recognize institutions that have shown three years of sustained improvement in student success. Colleges receiving this designation are expected to mentor other colleges in the ATD national network. In a similar fashion the Aspen Institute's Prize for Community College Excellence was established to recognize exceptional results achieved at leading institutions. Both Aspen and ATD should be lauded for shining a light on practices that appear to make a difference in completion rates; however, recognition begs an important question: To what extent are promising practices being implemented and scaled to the nation's community colleges?

The Center for Community College Student Engagement (CCCSE), drawing on regular surveys conducted at colleges nationally, provides insight about impactful practices from the perspective of students, faculty, and staff. In *A Matter of Degrees: Practices to Pathways*, CCCSE profiled high-impact practices, the extent to which these practices have been adopted by colleges, and the percentage of students who make use of the

Table 6.1.   Center for Community College Student Engagement High-Impact Practices

High-impact practice	Colleges Offering Practice (%)	Students Surveyed Taking Advantage of Practice (%)	
		All	Entering
Academic goal setting and planning	66	46	43
Orientation	97	60	66
Accelerated/fast-track development education	68	21	29
First-year experience	61	25	29
Student success course	84	20	29
Learning community	54	12	5
Experiential learning beyond classrooms	67 CTE programs 27 non-CTE programs	16	N/A
Tutoring	99	27	19
Supplemental instruction	61	20	31
Class attendance policy	76	76	76
Early alert and intervention	80	25	33

Source: Adapted from Center for Community College Engagement. Center for Community College Engagement, *A Matter of Degrees: Practices to Pathways* (Austin, TX: Center for Community College Engagement, 2014).

services provided by these colleges. Table 6.1 summarizes CCCSE's findings regarding impactful practices.[8]

Examining this table closely, it is clear that certain practices are more prevalent at some colleges than others. For instance, nearly all of the colleges CCCSE surveyed have practices related to orientation and tutoring compared with only 60 percent of colleges that had policies or programs in place for the first-year experience and supplemental instruction. This disparity isn't surprising, but given the strong evidence surrounding the effectiveness of interventions like learning communities and supplemental instruction, one would expect a higher percentage of colleges to have these practices in place.[9]

Perhaps more alarming than the lower percentage of colleges that offer critical student supports is the fact that across nearly all categories of high-impact practices CCCSE examined, a significantly smaller percentage of students take advantage of supports even if the college offers them. For example, fewer than 30 percent of new or continuing students surveyed indicated that they took a student success course during their first term, despite the fact that 84 percent of the colleges surveyed offer student success courses to students. Similarly, 21 percent of all students (and 29 percent of entering students) indicated that they took accelerated developmental education courses even though 68 percent of the colleges surveyed offer them. These are troubling statistics suggesting that it will be difficult to increase retention and completion rates if more students do not take advantage of proven strategies. The question is: Why are students not taking advantage of these opportunities?[10]

To be fair, some of these practices are more than likely targeted to specific student groups. For example, some colleges only promote student success courses to students who are placed in developmental education when they initially enroll. Alternatively, students may not know about the supports available because colleges do not adequately promote them. Kay McClenney, special advisor to the CEO of AACC and former director of CCCSE, is fond of saying, "students don't do optional." Unfortunately, many colleges don't make evidence-based interventions and practices mandatory. As a result, students don't avail themselves of the opportunity even though a particular intervention could help them achieve success. McClenney argues that colleges should *require* these interventions, especially for students who exhibit risk factors.

The reasons why institutions do not make success practices mandatory are complex. Limited resources certainly play a role, but this circumstance reflects a lack of scale that is a source of frustration for foundations, policymakers, and other reform-minded players. This dynamic is at the root of a growing trend by states to adopt outcomes-based funding formulas to create incentives for colleges to adopt high-impact success practices. The push by policymakers for improved outcomes is an important undertaking; however, all too frequently policies adopted to apply pressure to colleges are not developed in the most effective manner. Narrowing the gap between well-intended policymakers and practitioners will be a critical step in creating conditions for students to succeed.

WELL-INTENDED REFORMERS TALK PAST ONE ANOTHER

Practitioners have learned much more about students than was known ten years ago. In community colleges there is a deeper understanding of where students are falling out of the system, which in turn pinpoints strategies to retain them. State policymakers have stopped focusing exclusively on higher education appropriations and capital construction and instead are raising critical questions about college readiness, transfer, and articulation as a means to better align expectations across educational sectors. And yet, despite the "maturity" of the completion agenda, reformers at state and institutional levels continue to talk past one another.

To illustrate this point, the thrust and content of two recent national convenings (attended by the author) are highlighted. The first meeting was focused on developing higher education policy leadership, and the second was focused on the success of men of color. In both instances the overarching emphasis was on increasing completion rates and improving student outcomes, but the substance of these two meetings could not have been further apart.

The policy convening focused on identifying public policy prescriptions and the leadership capacity within state higher education agencies and system offices to improve success. The agenda stressed state-level strategic planning, academic quality, and outcomes-based funding formulas. There was virtually no discussion about students who are underprepared for college or the implications of policy prescriptions on access and success in postsecondary education for this population.

The agenda of the second conference focused on factors that contribute to poor completion rates among African American males, including the sociological, psychological, and organizational barriers they face and leadership interventions needed to reverse this trend. There was no discussion at this meeting about political and policy pressures colleges and universities face relative to the at-risk population and students more likely to complete. These meetings are highlighted not because conference gatherings should cover the waterfront of issues related to completion. They are contrasted as a means of pointing out a larger issue—the wide gap between policymakers and practitioners at the time we need to narrow it.

Individuals advocating for equity as part of the completion agenda point to solutions that address nuanced issues such as noncognitive or affective factors that inhibit student success. Advocates leading the charge on state policy change tend to boil reforms down to a handful of easy-to-grasp "game changing" strategies that oversimplify complex issues impacting student progression and success. Both approaches have value, but the disconnect between them is jarring and may be counterproductive to the shared goal of completion. The question is: How do we rectify the gap between policy and practice?

We can start by going back to the data. From the beginning, proponents of the completion agenda have pressed for setting clear attainment goals, which would be achieved through implementation of strategic plans. There has been a substantial amount of goal setting activity at the institutional, state, and national levels. The Lumina Foundation's goal—60 percent of the population having a postsecondary credential by 2025—is perhaps the most prominent. As noted previously, many states have articulated attainment goals that closely resemble Lumina's and have outlined the gap between current attainment and the level they would like to reach.[11]

To realistically achieve attainment goals, however, collective effort will be needed across all demographic groups. The challenge is that those who are more likely to succeed are already doing reasonably well.

As a result, meeting attainment goals will require more low-income, underrepresented, and first-generation students to succeed. Importantly, as our society becomes more diverse, a larger percentage of students will fall into one or all of these categories. We need to guard against having a deficit mindset about specific subgroups of students, but practitioners worry that policy prescriptions like outcomes-based funding and restrictions on academic remediation, while well intended, may create incentives for institutions to narrow access to at-risk populations. To avoid this result, a sustained dialogue needs to occur in states and among institutions. The next section presents a model that has emerged in a number of states to provide venues for dialogue and to thoughtfully address the gap between policy and practice.

CREATING STATE-LEVEL CAPACITY TO BRING COHERENCE TO THE COMPLETION AGENDA

Ten years ago, national meetings involving reformers underscored how little policymakers knew about community college students and what should be done to retain them, to say nothing of helping them persist to completion. Early initiatives—particularly ATD—did not have the benefit of knowledge and understanding generated by experimentation and evaluation of the past decade. While ATD was appropriately designed to focus on both institutional improvement and state policies that need to be in place to support individual institution efforts, the lack of evidence created a circumstance in which state and institutional efforts were not connected or aligned. This disconnect was exacerbated by the differing roles and responsibilities of numerous national intermediaries serving as partners in ATD.

Following a decade of national completion efforts, many state agencies and institutions are feeling the weight of initiative fatigue. For those that have been involved in numerous initiatives, financial support and technical expertise have been a welcome contribution. The dizzying array of reporting requirements, data requests, expectations, and timelines, however, have created challenges to making sense of the activity. Too often similar but distinct initiatives have operated in silos rather than aligned conversations in which the sum would become greater than the individual parts. This dynamic has played out at individual colleges and across campuses in states that have received substantial support from foundations.

At the other end of the spectrum, states and colleges outside the target locale of the national foundations or not directly involved in one of the marquee initiatives have struggled to gain access to information and expertise that more fortunate peers have received. In both circumstances, the question of scaling promising practices from investment, piloting, and research has been a challenge.

Community colleges are in a very different place today regarding what to do to improve student outcomes. While there are many questions unanswered, practitioners know a lot more about students and interventions that contribute to success. What has been lacking until recently are vehicles for disseminating knowledge, helping colleges adopt *and* adapt promising practices, and implementing them in way that is both sustainable and scalable to all colleges. One key example of a vehicle that has emerged to address this gap is statewide Student Success Centers.

Over the past several years, thirteen states have established Student Success Centers (SSC). The overarching role of SSCs, purposefully situated at the intersection of policy and practice, is to work with colleges on a state-by-state basis to bring coherence to initiatives underway and to advance lessons from the past decade of reform. With the national convergence around innovative practices and policy as a background, this new model of state-level intervention initially developed organically in four states (Arkansas, Michigan, Ohio, and Texas). In each of these states, community college associations were wrestling with how to better support the efforts of member colleges to address growing pressure to improve student outcomes and bring focus to the plethora of completion initiatives. Each association sought and received funding from the Kresge Foundation to launch a Student Success Center.[12]

With the early SSCs emerging largely independently of one another, the Kresge Foundation also funded Jobs for the Future (JFF) to facilitate a cross-state network of centers and to document the manner in which they were structured, the activities they were engaged in, and challenges they encountered. These efforts culminated in a 2013 JFF brief—*Joining Forces*—that outlined lessons from the early SSCs.[13]

At a basic level, SSCs organize regional community colleges around common action to leverage and accelerate efforts to improve student persistence and completion. They provide the vision, support, and a shared venue for community colleges working in partnership on a student success agenda. In respective states, SSCs take the lead in communicating to institutional stakeholders the components of a broad completion agenda and in building a coherent approach to engagement and policy advocacy across two-year institutions. Drawing from JFF's *Joining Forces* brief, the primary functions of a statewide Student Success Center include:

- *Convening and engagement:* Bring colleges together around reform; develop faculty leadership; create in-state networks and communities of practice; advance cross-sector alignment and collaboration; attend national convenings

- *Student success strategy alignment and coherence:* Map and align institutional, state, and national student success initiatives relevant to the state and its community colleges; create an umbrella framework and marshal necessary resources to accelerate the completion agenda
- *Data use to guide priorities and investments:* Improve data usage through work including metrics, sharing, transparency, coherence of metrics across initiatives, and increased IR capacity
- *Research and knowledge management:* Organize and synthesize evidence on models and their performance from in-state and national sources; make the information easily accessible to college innovators; map visible institutional strategies and their outcomes; develop newsletters, policy briefs, and overviews of individual or multicollege initiatives
- *Policy development and advocacy:* Specify and sharpen agendas for system and legislative change that promotes completion; identify and coordinate policy research needs; deepen state-level capacity for reform through mobilization of evidence and college voices; assist institutions with assessment of policy changes necessary at institutional, system, and state levels, corresponding to completion goals and strategies.[14]

Building on the efforts of early SSCs, the Kresge Foundation (2013) funded a national request for proposals, which was managed by Jobs for the Future, to establish three additional centers. The states selected (California, Connecticut, and New Jersey) emerged from a process that saw twenty-four states submit proposals in response to the RFP. With the SSC network growing to seven states and significant interest on the part of other states, the Bill and Melinda Gates Foundation collaborated with the Kresge Foundation in 2015 to fund a supplemental RFP process to further expand the network. SSCs were established in Hawaii, New York, North Carolina, Virginia, and Washington. Most recently, the Ford Family Foundation and the Oregon Community Foundation provided a grant to establish a center in Oregon as well.[15]

Host organizations in thirteen states, highlighted in table 6.2, are seeking to bridge the gap between policymakers and practitioners and unify colleges around a common agenda and peer–learning program. The SSCs combine a laser-like focus on sharing and disseminating evidence-based innovations at the institutional level with a commitment to aligning statewide success initiatives into a clear completion agenda.

Designed to support efforts to improve student outcomes at community colleges, the SSCs have emerged as a powerful infrastructure for change and innovation in states where they have been launched. States with SSCs work with nearly half of all public two-year colleges in the country. These institutions enrolled 58 percent of students in community

Table 6.2.   **States with Student Success Centers and Their Colleges**

State	Year Established	Host Organization	Public Two-Year Colleges	Fall Enrollment (2013–14)
AR	2010	Arkansas Community Colleges	22	55,985
CA	2014	Foundation for California Community Colleges	114	1,465,400
CT	2014	Connecticut Board of Regents for Higher Education	12	57,059
HI	2016	University of Hawai'i Community Colleges	7	28,455
MI	2011	Michigan Community College Association	30	222,286
NJ	2014	New Jersey Council of County Colleges	19	167,580
NY	2016	State University of New York	38	327,969
NC	2016	North Carolina Community College System	58	240,116
OH	2012	Ohio Association of Community Colleges	24	185,059
OR	2016	Oregon Community College Association	17	103,177
TX	2013	Texas Association of Community Colleges	65	695,601
VA	2016	Virginia Community College System	24	190,545
WA	2016	Washington State Board for Community and Technical Colleges	25	130,297
		Total in States with SSCs	453	3,872,053
		U.S. Total	934	6,678,073
		SSCs as a % of the U.S.	49	58

Source: IPEDS. National Center for Education Statistics, *Integrated Postsecondary Education Data System* (Washington, DC: U.S. Department of Education, Institute of Education Sciences, 2016).

colleges in the 2013–14 academic year. Significantly, over half (55 percent) of Pell Grant recipients and 67 percent of minority students were enrolled in SSC colleges in 2013–14, providing a channel to impact a substantial percentage of populations that have been historically disadvantaged. As these data indicate, the potential reach of existing Student Success Centers is considerable, and this has contributed to increased interest in their role as a vehicle for scaling innovation.

As intermediaries that work with colleges on a statewide basis, SSCs are influential in advancing the completion agenda that is grassroots in nature. Nowhere is this more evident than with the burgeoning focus on guided pathways. All of the Student Success Centers have either launched or are planning to launch a sustained multiyear effort focused on guided pathways. These pathways initiatives have surfaced in part as an organic response to local demand by colleges. The next section describes the guided pathways movement in more detail. Worth noting here is the ability of SSCs as state-based organizations to disseminate promising practices as part of the completion agenda.

GUIDED PATHWAYS: OVERARCHING FRAMEWORK FOR INSTITUTIONAL TRANSFORMATION

Ten years of intense reform efforts directed toward student success have led to promising shifts in the field. Awareness and commitment to completion have increased dramatically, colleges have greatly improved their capacity to use data to track student progress, and an expanding research and knowledge agenda related to student outcomes has yielded evidence colleges need to justify reforms. While most colleges are making needed changes and achieving improved outcomes, the field has lacked an overarching framework, which most, if not all, colleges can rally around to disseminate and scale evidence-based innovations. The guided pathways approach has emerged as this framework.

Drawing on the experience of Completion by Design and Achieving the Dream, guided pathways represent more than a simple catchphrase. They are an acknowledgment that, while progress has been made, it has been slow and limited to a small proportion of students. Guided pathways call for holistic, transformative change at institutions rather than isolated interventions involving small numbers of students. Recognizing these dynamics, national foundations have coalesced around guided pathways as a defining framework for action.

The most prominent guided pathway effort is the American Association of Community Colleges's Pathways Project. Working with national partners—Achieving the Dream, Aspen Institute, the Center for Community College Student Engagement, the Community College Research Center, Jobs for the Future, the National Center for Inquiry and Improvement, and Public Agenda—AACC launched this effort in 2015. The Pathways Project evolved from recommendations articulated in AACC's 21st-Century Commission on the Future of Community Colleges report, *Reclaiming the American Dream*.[16]

With funding from the Bill and Melinda Gates Foundation, the core of the Pathways Project involves a series of six institutes running through 2018 for thirty competitively chosen colleges. The specifics of this project are described in more detail later in this section. It is useful to first delve more deeply into the Pathways Model articulated by AACC.

The research undergirding guided pathways generally and AACC's guided pathways model specifically is best articulated in the Community College Research Center's recent book, *Redesigning America's Community Colleges*. CCRC suggests that institutions need to move away from a "cafeteria" service model that has been prevalent since the 1960s. The dramatic growth in the number of community colleges in the 1960s and 1970s was in response to increased demand for access to higher education. To meet expanding demand, the cafeteria model was the most expedient method to deliver an array of services to an increasingly diverse student population. This model did not, however, lend itself to increasing the number of students completing credentials with labor market value.[17]

Currently, too many colleges offer incoherent programs of study that present students with too many choices and too little support to make educated decisions. Furthermore, community colleges historically have had limited systems and processes in place for monitoring student progress toward educational goals, to say nothing of coherent methods for assessing the quality of learning in programs of study. In the current environment labor market demand is increasingly defining the value of academic credentials. When this dynamic is coupled with the skyrocketing cost of higher education, it is simply not ethical (or sustainable) for colleges to offer students ill-defined or poorly supported programs of study. This is particularly true for the many first-generation students who attend community colleges with little or no schema for making well-informed choices.[18]

Guided pathways provide a solution, but what is it? AACC defines the Pathways Model in the following way:

> The Pathways Model is an *integrated, institution-wide* approach to student success based on intentionally designed, clear, coherent and structured educational experiences, informed by available evidence, that guide each student effectively and efficiently from her/his point of entry through to attainment of high-quality postsecondary credentials and careers with value in the labor market.[19]

A primary lesson learned from early Achieving the Dream colleges was that they focused on isolated aspects of the student experience and/or on narrow subgroups of students. The Pathways Model is not a discrete intervention targeting a small number of students; rather, it is holistic reform of the way colleges do business. The AACC Pathways Model continues:

> Central to the pathways model are clear, educationally coherent program maps—which include specific course sequences, progress milestones, and program learning outcomes—that are aligned to what will be expected of

students upon program completion in the workforce and in education at the next level in a given field. Students are helped from the start to explore academic and career options, choose a program of study, and develop a plan based on the program maps. These plans simplify student decision-making, and they enable colleges to provide predictable schedules, frequent feedback, and targeted support as needed to help students stay on track and complete their programs more efficiently.[20]

Research suggests that it is a combination of many factors that contribute to student success. Some of these factors relate to individual students that institutions cannot control, but others are factors that colleges can control. Colleges have sought to remedy shortcomings, but changes have too often happened in isolation. The Pathways Model integrates institutional redesign features into a comprehensive approach to student support.

While the model combines a complex series of elements, it does so through a set of "essential practices and capacities," which are highlighted in table 6.3. These practices center on defining clear programs of study, helping students choose a path, putting supports in place to keep them on a chosen path, and ensuring that they are learning. These practices are simply stated, but they encompass substantial change that will need to take place on campuses. Redesign will not come easily. Community colleges will need to enhance their capacity in key areas: leadership, engagement, professional development, data availability and usage, and technology.[21]

Via the Pathways Model, AACC and its partnering organizations have organized a series of Pathways Institutes beginning in 2016 and concluding in 2018 that support the work of selected colleges "that demonstrate serious commitment to transformational work at scale." Thirty selected colleges send five-person teams to each of the institutes, where they work in-depth with national experts on a range of issues related to the essential practices and capacities summarized above. The colleges receive ongoing support from national partners as well as a team of coaches assigned to each institution.

Beyond the connection to colleges directly participating in the Pathways Project, an important goal of the project is to build understanding in the field about implementation of the Pathways Model. To support knowledge development, AACC, its partner organizations, and the thirty colleges involved are engaged in ongoing, multipronged research over the course of the institutes. Project leadership is also providing open access to all the materials, tools, and templates developed through the project. Another critical outcome of this project is the development of a corps of practitioners who have worked on issues and challenges related to the adoption of pathways. Practitioners can, in turn, become

Table 6.3.   AACC Pathways Model Essential Practices and Essential Capacities

Essential Practices

Dimension #1: Clarify paths to student end goals
- Simplify students' choices with default program maps that show students a clear pathway to completion, further education, and employment in fields of importance to the region
- Establish transfer pathways through alignment of pathway courses and expected learning outcomes with transfer institutions

Dimension #2: Help students choose and enter a pathway
- Bridge K–12 to higher education by assuring early remediation in the final year of high school
- Redesign traditional remediation as an "on ramp" to a program of study
- Provide accelerated remediation to help *very poorly prepared* students succeed in college-level courses as soon as possible

Dimension #3: Help students stay on path
- Support students through a strong advising process, embedded and ongoing in the pathway experience and supported by appropriate technology
- Embed academic and nonacademic supports throughout students' programs to promote student learning and persistence

Dimension #4: Ensure that students are learning
- Establish program-level learning outcomes aligned with the requirements for success in employment and further education
- Integrate group projects, internships, and other applied learning experiences to enhance instruction and student success in courses across programs of study
- Ensure incorporation of effective teaching practice throughout the pathways

Essential Capacities

- Leadership demonstrating skills for managing and sustaining large-scale transformational change
- Broad and authentic engagement of college faculty and staff—particularly advisors—in the design, implementation, evaluation, and ongoing improvement of pathways for students
- Institutional will and capacity to use data and evidence to design academic and career pathways, monitor student progress, and implement needed improvements over time
- Technological tools and infrastructure appropriate to support student progress through guided pathways
- Commitment to the level of strategically targeted professional development that will be required to design and implement pathways at scale
- Policy conditions established at the state, governing board, system, and institutional level that provide incentives, structures, and supports for pathway design and implementation at scale while removing barriers
- A continuing action research agenda that examines the efficacy of guided pathways and develops practical knowledge and tools to support effective implementation at scale

Source: Adapted from the AACC Pathways Model. American Association of Community Colleges, *The Pathway Project* (Washington, DC: American Association of Community Colleges, 2016).

part of a growing national network of experts that help to inform/support colleges in reform efforts.

An important aspect of the Pathways Institutes and Student Success Centers is alignment of their work with Gates Foundation funding. On the surface level, there is already significant alignment among the seventeen states where the thirty AACC Pathways colleges are located. Eighteen of these colleges are located in eight states with Student Success Centers. All of the Student Success Centers have launched or are contemplating a pathways initiative. Several states (Michigan, Ohio, North Carolina, Texas, Virginia, and Washington) have statewide institutes underway that are conceptually similar to the AACC Pathways Project Institutes.

Efforts in all of these states have informed how the national institutes were designed and have drawn on the lessons, tools, and materials developed by AACC and its partners. More pointedly, Texas and Washington have partnered directly with AACC to develop multiyear pathway institutes that closely replicate the national model. Partners involved in the AACC Project are also working with individual Student Success Centers to provide technical assistance. Alignment between the AACC Pathways Project and the Student Success Centers is encouraging, but this alone will not supply the technical assistance required in the field to improved institutional performance and elevate student outcomes. The last section of this chapter will discuss how broad ecosystem reform must be carried out to achieve this goal.

EMBEDDING STATE AND INSTITUTIONAL EFFORTS WITHIN A LARGER ECOSYSTEM OF REFORM

Over the past decade of reform, state community college systems and higher education coordinating/governing boards have shifted policy and incentive structures toward student outcomes. State policies have been enacted to change institutional behavior. Reacting to pressure from political leaders, state higher education systems have established statewide completion agendas to define attainment goals and to measure and fund student outcomes. State agencies are working diligently to implement directives from governors and legislators, but all too often these efforts fall short because agencies are not designed or equipped to perform a sustained convening role around the dissemination and implementation of promising practices at individual colleges. System offices and higher education agencies historically have been compliance entities and even if they have adequate staffing are not designed to help institutions scale reform. Rarely do they provide needed professional development opportunities for faculty and administrators to implement innovative practices.

National leaders of reform conversations lament that the public does not know about exemplary practices at leading colleges like Valencia College, City Colleges of Chicago, or Walla Walla Community College. Unfortunately, outcomes-based funding will not create connections across institutions. It will take an intentional strategy and infrastructure to support this work on the ground. This is a primary reason why so many states are interested in creating Student Success Centers to bridge the gap between capacity and knowledge and between the efforts of policymakers and practitioners.

These centers are positioned as a parallel activity working in concert with state policy dialogues. They can be housed within a state agency or in a community college association, but the two need to be strategically aligned and reinforce one another. Policy should push institutional reform and institutional reform should inform modifications in policy. Political leadership will continue to push top-down policy change, but a corollary state-level conversation (through entities like the centers) is needed to guide change and scale across institutions. This is a nuanced view that policymakers and funders are coming to appreciate, and the Student Success Centers are providing a much-needed answer to the longstanding dilemma of bridging the gap between policy and practice.

The Student Success Centers by themselves, however, cannot lead to the transformation of colleges individually and collectively. Successful transformation depends on three components that need to be integrated into the larger ecosystem of reform: 1) examples, or proof points, of what institutional reform can look like; 2) leadership distributed throughout colleges that promotes change and risk taking; and 3) continuing technical assistance and expertise to help states and colleges navigate change.

One of the key outcomes of the AACC Pathways Institutes is creation of proof points of exemplary practices that colleges can adopt and high-performing institutions they can emulate. Key, however, will be a vehicle for making the experience of exemplar colleges readily available to others. National partners and funders will need to work in a coordinated fashion to provide seamless and ongoing support to colleges as they go about the hard work of transformation. Some partners and structures lend themselves to breadth of scale, while others are better suited to provide deeper technical support.

For example, the Student Success Centers are designed to aggregate the actions and needs of colleges in their state, but they are not designed to provide intensive institutional coaching. AACC's Pathways Institutes work more intensively and provide support networks for colleges as they wrestle with the work of guided pathways. Achieving the Dream and the National Center for Inquiry and Improvement are both engaged in ongoing coaching for individual colleges that is at a level of engagement that neither the Pathways Institutes nor the Student Success Centers are designed to provide. The key to scale will be to provide breadth and depth of support in a coordinated fashion and to sustain it over time.

NOTES

1. National Center for Higher Education Management Systems, *State Policies and Practices Consistent with the National Attainment Agenda* (Boulder, CO: National Center for Higher Education Management Systems, 2014); Alene Russell, *A Guide to Major U.S. College Completion Initiatives* (Washington, DC: American Association of State Colleges and Universities, 2010).

2. Lumina Foundation, *A Stronger Nation 2016* (Indianapolis, IN: Lumina Foundation, 2016).

3. Kelly Field, "6 Years in and 6 to Go, Only Modest Progress on Obama's College-Completion Goal," *The Chronicle of Higher Education*, January 20, 2015.

4. 21st-Century Commission on the Future of Community Colleges, *Reclaiming the American Dream: Community Colleges and the Nation's Future* (Washington, DC: American Association of Community Colleges, 2012); American Association of Community Colleges, *College Completion Challenge: A Call to Action* (Washington, DC: American Association of Community Colleges, 2012).

5. American Association of Community Colleges, *Community College Completion: Progress toward Goal of 50% Increase* (Washington, DC: American Association of Community Colleges, 2015).

6. Elizabeth Zachry Rutschow, Lashawn Richburg-Hayes, Thomas Brock, Genevieve Orr, Oscar Cerna, Dan Cullinan, Monica Reid Kerrigan, Davis Jenkins, Susan Gooden, and Kasey Martin, *Turning the Tide: Five Years of Achieving the Dream in Community Colleges* (New York: MDRC and Community College Research Center, 2011).

7. Ibid.

8. Center for Community College Student Engagement, *A Matter of Degrees: Practices to Pathways* (Austin, TX: Center for Community College Student Engagement, The University of Texas at Austin, 2014).

9. Ibid.

10. Ibid.

11. Lumina Foundation, *A Stronger Nation 2016*; National Center for Higher Education Management Systems, National Center for Higher Education Management Systems, *State Policies and Practices Consistent with the National Attainment Agenda*.

12. Jobs for the Future, *Student Success Center Network* (Boston, MA: Jobs for Future), accessed October 1, 2016, http://www.jff.org/initiatives/postsecondary-state-policy/student-success-center-network.

13. Lara K. Couturier, *Joining Forces: How Student Success Centers Are Accelerating Statewide Community College Improvement Efforts* (Boston, MA: Jobs for Future, 2013).

14. Ibid.

15. Jobs for the Future, *Student Success Center Network*.

16. American Association of Community Colleges, *The Pathways Project* (Washington, DC: American Association of Community Colleges), accessed October 1, 2016, http://www.aacc.nche.edu/Resources/aaccprograms/pathways/Pages/default.aspx.

17. Thomas R. Bailey, Shanna Smith Jaggars, and Davis Jenkins, *Redesigning America's Community Colleges: A Clearer Path to Student Success* (Cambridge, MA: Harvard University Press, 2015).

18. Ibid.

19. American Association of Community Colleges, *The Pathways Project*.

20. Ibid.

21. Ibid.

SEVEN

Implications of the Completion Agenda for Equity and Quality

A Question of Resources

The closing section of the book returns to implications of the completion agenda on equity and quality introduced in the prologue. This discussion pointedly raises questions about whether community colleges are adequately resourced to realize the attainment of ambitious goals policymakers, foundations, and the colleges themselves have set. In an era of constrained resources, the answer to challenges posed by the completion agenda cannot simply be more money. However, given the propensity of a diverse population to enroll in community colleges and the outsized role these institutions play in meeting attainment goals, it would seem appropriate to ask questions about how effectively public resources are being used to support community college students.

ACCESS VERSUS SUCCESS OR ACCESS AND SUCCESS?

In January 2015 the Obama administration put forward a proposal for two years of free community college for anyone who wants it. The America's Promise Scholarship proposal, which was modeled on a similar program in Tennessee, is intended to provide students that enroll at least part time, maintain a 2.5 grade point average, and make steady progress toward completion a scholarship to cover the cost of tuition.[1] This proposal follows a series of gatherings hosted by the White House focused on higher education. In January 2014 Barack Obama convened a summit on college access. To be invited, attendees were obliged to make a formal commitment to improve access for low-income and underrepresented students.

For community college proponents, the free community college proposal and the summits on college access have a familiar ring. Community colleges have been an affordable access point for millions of Americans entering postsecondary education. In many ways, community colleges have already answered the president's call. Many low-income students are already eligible for the full Pell Grant, which would cover most, if not all, of the cost of tuition and fees at community colleges throughout the nation.

The more significant financial hurdle for students lies in the cost of attendance beyond tuition such as housing, transportation, childcare, etc. These expenses are not covered by the Pell Grant or by various promise scholarships that have been proposed. As a result, students are forced take student loans and/or work full or part time to cover supplemental expenses. Analyses suggest that students from higher-income brackets will benefit most from the promised scholarship programs, despite the fact that they do not need "free" college to attend. Free college proposals, while well-intended efforts to provide greater access to college, might divert limited resources toward populations who would otherwise attend college and away from investment in enhanced student supports that research suggests are the key to student progression and completion.

A continuing focus on access is critical, yet it comes after a decade of reform efforts fixated on completion and success. Community colleges have been under increased scrutiny from the Obama administration, foundations, and state policymakers about student outcomes—particularly in terms of the credentials they earn and the jobs they secure. The focus on student progression and completion has challenged fundamental assumptions about how community colleges operate, what their mission is, and how to improve outcomes. The growing emphasis on success has also been accompanied by an intensifying accountability mandate in the form of outcomes-based funding. As a result, colleges are being pushed to make strategic choices that could actually work to limit access.

The Obama administration is on the right track in illuminating issues about student access. It has also been appropriate for the president to push student success early in his administration. After ten years of reform efforts, colleges are examining student progression more closely. A deep dive into data about student progression and completion has led to inevitable questions about the sustainability of the open-access mission. With policymakers and foundations expecting community colleges to produce more graduates, institutions are changing the way they operate. The overarching question is whether or not the changes colleges and states are pursuing to increase completion rates will limit access for those less likely to succeed. In an era of constrained resources and rising expectations for outcomes, it is incumbent on community college leaders to balance these competing priorities.

REAL-WORLD APPLICATION OF
COMPETING INSTITUTIONAL LOGICS

Chapter 2 focused on institutional logics—the beliefs and practices within a profession that guide action through collective identity and categories of behavior. Central to the institutional logics framework is the notion that a dominant logic can be challenged and ultimately changed over time. In community colleges, the dominant access logic has reinforced the long-held view that open admissions institutions maximize opportunity and convenience through a wide range of programs and course offerings. The shift toward an emergent logic accentuating the importance of outcomes and success raises critical questions about the students community colleges serve and the resources required to adequately support them. As the lens changes from enrollment to credential attainment, a markedly different "set of material practices" is required of colleges as well as a different approach to strategy.[2]

The American Association of Community Colleges's 21st-Century Commission report, *Reclaiming the American Dream*, highlights the shift colleges need to make between the access logic and the success logic. The report calls on colleges to change their culture from one that is tolerant of achievement gaps, relies on anecdotes, and allows work to happen in isolation to one that is committed to closing achievement gaps, embraces evidence-based practices, and promotes collaboration. The following seven recommendations from this report will transform institutions from a focus on access and getting students in the door to helping students succeed in their educational goals:

1. Increase completion rates by 50 percent by 2020.
2. Dramatically improve college readiness.
3. Close the American skills gaps.
4. Refocus the community college mission and redefine institutional roles.
5. Invest in collaborative support structures.
6. Target public and private investments strategically.
7. Implement policies and practices that promote rigor and accountability.[3]

These are laudable goals, and the association is to be commended for putting forth such ambitious objectives for community colleges. AACC could have walked a well-worn path of self-interested entities pointing fingers at factors beyond its control rather than embracing the shortcoming of the colleges and advocating change. The association's leadership chose not to do this, and the goals espoused in *Reclaiming the American Dream* should be taken quite seriously as a result. That said, stating ambitious goals and making the shift from the historical focus on access to one of access *and* success will be daunting.

COMMUNITY COLLEGES: SEPARATE AND UNEQUAL?

Resources constraints are a significant barrier to colleges pursuing ambitious completion goals adopted by AACC. The Great Recession in 2009 and 2010 resulted in dramatic cuts in state funding for public colleges and universities. While state appropriations have recovered since then, according to a 2016 report from the Center for Budget and Policy Priorities, funding for public two- and four-year colleges is still $8.7 billion below prerecession levels. The 2016 version of the *State Higher Education Finance* report produced by the State Higher Education Executive Officers expands on this point. The report indicates that over a twenty-five-year period, per FTE appropriations declined from a high of $9,120 in 2001 to $6,966 in 2015. During the same period, the growing dependence on tuition is also clear with net tuition revenue per FTE increasing from $3,801 in 2001 to $6,006 in 2015.[4]

Analyses conducted by AACC mirror these trends and indicate that state funding for community colleges has declined by six percentages points since the 2008–9 academic year. The revenue lost from state appropriations has largely been replaced by tuition dollars. More specifically, in 2008 state appropriations represented approximately 36 percent of community college revenue, tuition was 24 percent, and the balance was a combination of local property tax, federal dollars, and miscellaneous revenue.

By the 2013–14 academic year, tuition and state appropriations were roughly even at 30 percent of the community college revenue picture nationally.[5] Compounding the challenge of community college reliance on tuition dollars in the past few years has been enrollment decline as the economy has improved and prospective students returned to work. Economic improvement is always desirable, but it forced colleges to adjust to lower tuition revenue or to increase tuition. Both of these scenarios are problematic, and they are exacerbated by disinvestment on the part of states.

Given ongoing fiscal constraints, colleges committed to improving student outcomes will have no choice but to change the way they do business. They will need to reallocate resources to provide comprehensive support and make tough choices about what they will or will not do. Critical institutional dialogues will need to happen. If policymakers, college leaders, opinion makers, etc. expect to see greater outcomes from these colleges, we need to find a new approach to finance them moving forward that ensures adequate resources for critical student supports.

The Century Foundation released a 2013 report titled *Bridging the Higher Education Divide* aimed at making a case for a new finance formula to stem stratification among colleges and universities. While other publications have highlighted issues related to stratification, this report is worthy of attention because it directly links the disparity in resources among colleges and universities to differences in student outcomes. This publication, which was the product of the twenty-three-person task force on Preventing Community Colleges from Becoming Separate and Unequal, presents two key recommendations:

- Create new outcomes-based funding in higher education, with a greater emphasis on providing additional public supports based on student needs; and
- Reduce racial and economic stratification between two- and four-year institutions.

These recommendations acknowledged that to meet President Obama's goal of increased educational attainment, eight million additional degrees would be required by 2020, five million of which would need to be produced by community colleges. The challenge, this report highlights, is that community colleges serve a student population with higher need, but have limited resources to provide adequate support. Community colleges are *separate* from other higher education institutions because of increasing stratification of students by race and socioeconomic status and comparatively *unequal* in terms of funding and student outcomes.[6]

More specifically, the Century Foundation report states that from 1982 to 2006, the proportion of students enrolled at community colleges from the bottom two income quartiles increased from 48 percent to 58 percent, while the percentage of students from the top two quartiles decreased from 52 percent to 43 percent. Stated differently, 70 percent of the students at elite institutions are from the highest income quartile, while only 5 percent are from the lowest income quartile. At community colleges, 28 percent of students from the lowest income quartile outnumber 16 percent of students from the highest quartile nearly two to one.[7]

The racial makeup of the community college student population has shifted markedly with the percentage of white students dropping from 73 percent in 1994 to 58 percent in 2006, while the percentage of black and Hispanic student increased from 21 to 33 percent over the same period. The shift in racial demographics between 1994 and 2006 was much less pronounced at elite higher education institutions. The percentage of white students at elite institutions dropped modestly from 78 percent to 75 percent, while the percentage of black and Hispanic students remained essentially unchanged—11 percent in 1994 and 12 percent in 2006.

The economic and demographic makeup of the community college student population is closely correlated with diminished student outcomes noted throughout the book. Conversely, outcomes at elite institutions, with a student population that is disproportionally white and economically better off, are significantly higher. Statistically, low-income and minority students are less likely to progress and complete a credential. An important factor at play for students of depressed backgrounds is the deficit in academic preparation when they arrive on campus. Simply put, they start further behind.

The Century Foundation report goes on to argue that a key factor in differential student outcomes between community colleges and other higher education institutions is the resources available to support students. According to the report, community colleges have considerably less funding per FTE than elite research institutions that enroll a disproportionally high percentage of students from more privileged backgrounds. The report notes that between 1999 and 2009 community colleges only saw a $1 increase in per FTE funding, while public research universities saw a $4,000 increase. This disparity is alarming on many levels, but more importantly it raises a question about how we can realistically consider a dramatic improvement in student outcomes in community colleges without addressing funding inequities—inequities that are clearly connected to societal inequity.[8]

To address the resource disparity between higher education institutions and mitigate the trend toward stratification among students enrolled in them, the Century Report leveled the following recommendations:

1. Adopt state and federal "adequacy"-based funding in higher education akin to that used in primary and secondary education, combined with considerations of outcomes.
2. Establish greater transparency in public financial subsidies to higher education.
3. Encourage the growth of redesigned institutions that facilitate a connection between community colleges and four-year colleges.
4. Take concrete steps to facilitate community college transfer.
5. Encourage innovation in racially and economically inclusive community college honors programs.
6. Encourage innovation in early college programs that enhance community college diversity.
7. Prioritize funding of new programs for economically and racially isolated community colleges.
8. Provide incentives for four-year institutions to engage in affirmative action for low-income students of all races.[9]

These recommendations would entail an important shift in how colleges and universities are funded and aligned. The "adequacy" proposal in particular, which calls for additional funding for economically disadvantaged students, would acknowledge and support the special role community colleges play in supporting state and federal attainment goals. This recommendation would need to be coupled with transparent accountability guidelines to ensure that additional resources are allocated to supports that research suggests are most likely to contribute to student success. An investment of this kind could be the missing ingredient necessary to help colleges adopt and scale promising practices that have emerged in the last decade of the reform movement.

As game changing as this investment strategy could be, making the case for additional resources to optimize student success will be difficult because of state budget constraints. Further, advocates of outcomes-based funding will argue that formulas adopted in the past decade should provide colleges with plenty of incentive to reallocate resources to meet the needs of underprepared students. The next section will explore if this is indeed the case.

IS OUTCOMES-BASED FUNDING THE ANSWER?

As stated in chapter 4, thirty-five states have adopted outcomes-based funding formulas in the past five to ten years. Early research by the Community College Research Center suggests that because most of the states only recently adopted outcomes-based formulas, more time is needed to adequately assess their effectiveness. However, another recent report from the Century Foundation pointedly states that performance-based funding doesn't lead to improved student outcomes in higher education, nor does it bring about improved results in the context of other public services. The report cites a set of twelve different academic studies measuring the effect of outcomes-based funding for colleges and universities. Among the studies cited, all but two had null or negative impact on outcomes, and those with a positive result were modest. The question is: Why?[10]

The Century Foundation report challenges three underlying assumptions that are frequently articulated by advocates of outcome-based funding—incentives encourage low-performing institutions to improve, a clear pathway is in place for achieving results, and effects will be sustained over time. Examination of assumptions individually reveals some of the flawed reasoning behind current approaches to outcomes-based funding.

First, colleges that are low performing by definition have more distance to travel for improvement compared to high-performing colleges. Depending on the manner in which funding incentives are structured, low performers may be competing against institutions better positioned to meet performance goals, thereby weakening their position to acquire funding. Furthermore, low-performing institutions may enroll a higher percentages of at-risk students that require additional resources—a cycle that is difficult to break.

The assumption that colleges know what to do to improve student outcomes is significantly flawed. While the reform movement of the past decade has raised awareness of practices and procedures that contribute to improved student outcomes, there is a large number of colleges in which faculty and staff simply do not have knowledge of the latest research on promising practices. Moreover, most educators are not versed in change management strategies to achieve scaled implementation of evidenced-based reforms.

Finally, the Century Foundation report suggests that sustaining performance gains can be difficult. This is true, in part, because colleges (and other public sector entities) often do not use performance data to make adjustments and continue to innovate. The past decade has seen major improvement in data capacity among community colleges, but this capacity is used sporadically and all too often end users who could most use the data don't have it. Further, community colleges are complex organizations that do not readily lend themselves to pinpoint state funding directed to discrete practices that need to be modified.[11]

An issue not raised in the Century Foundation report that may be limiting the impact of performance-based funding is that the amount of funding tied to these formulas is modest compared to total funding. HCM Strategists's 2015 report indicated that only five of the thirty-five states that adopted outcomes-based funding were allocating more than 10 percent of total higher education funding through the formula and twenty-five states allocated less than 5 percent of the total. Assuming colleges know what to do to improve, the limited percentage of funding in play with the formula may not provide adequate incentives for institutions to reallocate resources in a manner that makes a difference.[12]

As discussed in chapter 6, recent work by the Center for Community College Student Engagement found that colleges are not making key support services mandatory for all students or for targeted groups of at-risk students despite the evidence that suggests these services lead to better outcomes.[13] There may be other factors that impel colleges to make these choices, but sufficient resources to provide student supports make up a key driver. Advocates of outcomes-based funding formulas would argue that the incentives created by the formula will spur colleges to reallocate resources internally, but this is clearly not the case . . . at least not for now.

The Century Foundation report suggests that states should emphasize *capacity-building* and *equity-based funding* as alternatives to outcomes-based funding formulas to drive improvement in student outcomes. There is no question about a need to enhance institutional capacity through entities like the Student Success Centers discussed in chapter 6 or new "adequacy" funding structures acknowledging the inequity between higher education institutions. The political reality is that the accountability mindset behind outcomes-based funding formulas is not going to go away and the external pressure that stems from them is an important driver for colleges to improve performance. The question is how to ensure a balanced approach that does not exacerbate inequities or diminish quality.[14]

CLOSING THOUGHTS ON EQUITY AND QUALITY

The issues of equity and quality can certainly be treated as separate questions, but ensuring equity has never been about providing underserved populations with the chance to enroll in college. Nor has the focus on quality been exclusively for students fortunate enough to attend an elite institution. These issues are closely intertwined and, while the goal may never be fully realized, it is to provide all students with access to a quality education. The dichotomy of access versus success in community colleges is in the end really a false distinction. Students and families are not enrolling in and paying for college simply for the sake of it. Most students enroll with some semblance of a goal in mind—even if that goal isn't fully defined or informed. The role of open-access community colleges has always been to meet students where they are and move them toward their educational goal.

What we have learned in past decade is that students—especially those from disadvantaged backgrounds—all too often don't know what they want to do at a level that enables them to navigate a complex college environment. Add to this a circumstance in which institutions have not invested sufficient time and effort in systems, policies, and practices to help students make informed decisions and the result is, not surprisingly, low completion rates. The question of equity looms larger because gaps in outcomes are dramatically worse for low-income and minority students.

We have also learned in the past decade that quality isn't simply an abstract notion of what individual faculty judge to be significant. The views of the faculty are obviously important, but the unit of analysis for quality—for good or for ill—is increasingly the labor market demand for skills and the expertise students acquire. If the knowledge students attain while attending community colleges is misaligned with what is expected by employers, we are collectively doing a major disservice to students who are able to progress and complete a credential.

Much of this book has focused on strategies and tactics to change policy conditions, enhance institutional capacity, and to streamline programming. All of these strategies are a means to an end, and that end is to improve the prospect for students to have productive lives in which they can support families and thrive. Too often in deliberations about reform, practitioners lose sight of this simple reality and get hung up in the politics of the moment. There has been an incredible amount of progress over the past decade, but there is much that needs to be done. Many of the dialogues about student completion and success over the past decade have focused a lot on whether or not students are college ready. It is time to turn this question around and ask: "Are college students ready?" If we focus on this question, many seemingly important issues will melt away and we will have the opportunity to address root problems.

NOTES

1. "White House Unveils America's College Promise Proposal: Tuition-Free Community College for Responsible Students," White House, Office of the Press Secretary, last modified January 9, 2015, https://www.whitehouse.gov/the-press-office/2015/01/09/fact-sheet-white-house-unveils-america-s-college-promise-proposal-tuitio.

2. Roger Friedland and Robert R. Alford, "Bringing Society Back In: Symbols, Practices, and Institutional Contradictions," in *The New Institutionalism in Organizational Analysis*, ed. Walter W. Powell and Paul J. DiMaggio (Chicago: University of Chicago Press, 1991), 232–63, 248.

3. 21st-Century Commission on the Future of Community Colleges, *Reclaiming the American Dream: Community Colleges and the Nation's Future* (Washington, DC: American Association of Community Colleges, 2012).

4. Michael Mitchell, Michael Leachman, and Kathleen Masterson, *Funding Down, Tuition Up: State Cuts to Higher Education Threaten Quality and Affordability at Public Colleges* (Washington, DC: Center on Budget and Policy Priorities, 2016); State Higher Education Executive Officers, *State Higher Education Finance: Fiscal Year 2015* (Boulder, CO: State Higher Education Executive Officers, 2016).

5. Kent Phillippe, *Data Points: Where the Revenue Comes From* (Washington, DC: American Association of Community Colleges, 2016).

6. The Century Foundation Task Force on Preventing Community Colleges from Becoming Separate and Unequal, *Bridging the Higher Education Divide: Strengthening Community Colleges and Restoring the American Dream* (New York: The Century Foundation, 2013).

7. Ibid.

8. Ibid.

9. Ibid.

10. "Performance-Based Funding for Higher Education," *National Conference of State Legislatures*, last modified July 31, 2015, http://www.ncsl.org/research/educa

tion/performance-funding.aspx; Kevin J. Dougherty, Sosanya M. Jones, Hana Lahr, Rebecca S. Natow, Lara Pheatt, and Vikash Reddy, "Looking Inside the Black Box of Performance Funding for Higher Education: Policy Instruments, Organizational Obstacles, and Intended and Unintended Impacts," *The Russell Sage Foundation Journal of the Social Sciences* 2, no. 1 (2016): 147–73; Nicholas Hillman, *Why Performance-Based College Funding Doesn't Work* (New York: The Century Foundation, 2016).

11. Hillman, *Why Performance-Based College Funding Doesn't Work.*

12. Martha Snyder, *Driving Better Outcomes: Typology and Principles to Inform Outcomes-Based Funding Models* (Washington, DC: HCM Strategist, 2015).

13. Center for Community College Student Engagement, *A Matter of Degrees: Practices to Pathways* (Austin, TX: Center for Community College Student Engagement, The University of Texas at Austin, 2014).

14. Hillman, *Why Performance-Based College Funding Doesn't Work.*

Index

About the Author

Christopher Baldwin is senior director of state policy and network relations at Jobs for the Future. His work is focused on JFF's policy efforts, specifically related to improving student outcomes in postsecondary education. Returning to JFF in August 2015, Dr. Baldwin plays a leading role in efforts to expand the Student Success Centers Network. Leveraging nearly five years as the executive director of the Michigan Center for Student Success, Dr. Baldwin has supported the expansion of the Student Success Center Network to thirteen states. The centers are a state-level intermediary designed to share and spread evidence-based innovations across institutions, while also aligning myriad success initiatives into a coherent statewide completion agenda. Sitting at the intersection of policy and practice, the centers have emerged as critical infrastructure for change and innovation in states where they have been launched.

In his prior role with JFF, Dr. Baldwin co-directed the state policy component of Achieving the Dream and the Developmental Education Initiative. Through these initiatives, he worked with departments of higher education, community college system offices, and associations of community colleges in sixteen states providing strategic advice and technical assistance concerning the adoption of state policies that support and encourage improved outcomes for community college students.

Earning his doctorate in higher education administration from the Center for the Study of Higher and Postsecondary Education at the University of Michigan, Dr. Baldwin's research focuses on the tensions in community colleges between maintaining open-door access and simultaneously promoting degree completion. Dr. Baldwin has also served as vice president for government and community outreach at Owens Community College in northwest Ohio, where he worked on state and national policy affecting community colleges, and has served in a variety of governmental and advocacy positions over the past two decades, including a position in the office of the governor of the State of Ohio.

Dr. Baldwin lives with wife and three children in Dexter, Michigan.